GW00701901

IKEBANA AT HOME

IKEBANA AT HOME

Ruth Grosser

First published in 1993 by Boolarong Publications
With The Ikebana Centre, Australia, P.O. Box 1931, Southport, 4215.

National Library of Australia
Cataloguing-in-Publication data

Grosser, Ruth, 1944- .
Ikebana at home.
ISBN 0 646 14929 6.

1. Flower arrangement, Japanese. I. Ikebana Centre Australia.
II. Title.

745.92252

BOOLARONG PUBLICATIONS
12 Brookes Street, Bowen Hills, Brisbane, QLD. 4006
Design and phototypesetting by
Ocean Graphics Pty Ltd, Gold Coast, QLD.
Printed by Fergies Colour Printer, Brisbane.
Bound by Podlich Enterprises, Brisbane.
Colour Separation by Sphere Colour Graphics, Brisbane.

CONTENTS

DEDICATION

TO MY HUSBAND DAVID.

ABOUT THE AUTHOR

Ruth Grosser, B.A. B.Sc, 1st Grade Master, Sogetsu School, Master-Teacher, Ikenobo School.

Ruth Grosser was born in a country town in NS.W. Her family moved to Sydney when she was two years old. She was educated and attended University in Sydney. She worked as an Art Teacher for a time. She paints and sculpts as well as teaches Ikebana. She lived, with her husband and three children, in England for a number of years, and first saw Ikebana in England. When she returned to Australia she studied with Mr Norman Sparnon and Mrs Frieda Harrison and has studied in Japan for many years.

She was the founding President of the Gold Coast Chapter of Ikebana International, No. 229. This she founded in 1988, The Bi-Centennial Year of Australia. She was previously President of the Lismore Chapter, No 32. She was Vice-Chairman of the 15th Australian/New Zealand Regional Conference, which was held on the Gold Coast in 1985. She has lived on the Gold Coast, Queensland, since 1985, with her husband and children.

She runs the Ikebana Centre, Australia, on the Gold Coast.

She has represented Australian Chapters of I.I. at the 4th, 5th and 6th World Conventions in Japan and has exhibited Ikebana arrangements at The Sydney Art Gallery, Tokyo and Kyoto Exhibition Centres, Wellington and Christchurch N.Z., David Jones Dept. Stores, The Arts Centre, Gold Coast, Griffith University, Observation City Hotel, Perth, Hong Kong and Taipei, Taiwan.

She gives many Lectures and Demonstrations on Ikebana and is in demand as a Guest Speaker.

She will be Chairperson of the Australian/New Zealand Regional Conference to be held at the Gold Coast in 1995.

ACKNOWLEDGEMENTS

I would like to sincerely thank John Fisher, an excellent Photographer on the Gold Coast, for his professional photography.

My husband David and I have been married for 25 years this year, and I would like to dedicate this book to him and thank him for his constant support and love.

Many thanks to my friends and students, who have so generously opened their homes. Grethe and John Andersen, Barbara and Jack Collins, Adele and Charles Darmanin, Carol and John Hempstalk, Beverley and Alan Jones, Alison and Grant Kirkbeck, Jennie and Stewart McKay, and Solange and Yvan Ohlen.

My thanks must go also, to The Gold Coast City Art Gallery, The Sheraton-Mirage Hotel (Gold Coast) and The Royal Pines Hotel (A Prince Hotel – Gold Coast.)

To my children, Michelle, Mark and Andrew, thank you for your support and love.

The award-winning orchids were supplied by Karl and Ruth Wessely.

The Haiku poems were taken from two books entitled – "A Chime of Windbells" and "A Net of Fireflies"– Charles E. Tuttle: Publishers, Rutland, Vermont and Tokyo.

The New Guinea story of the Moka and Bilum was taken from the book "Paradise Tales", Published by Robert Brown and Assoc., (Aust) Pty. Ltd. P.O. Box 29, Bathurst, N.S.W.

PREFACE

"If a man find himself with bread in both hands, he should exchange one loaf for some flowers; since the loaf feeds the body indeed, but the flower feeds the soul." Anon.

Ikebana is a formative Art.

What is the meaning of the word Art? and Why is Ikebana Art?

"Art is Man added to Nature" . . . . Francis Bacon (1561-1626).

To some people, who haven't given much thought to what Art means, Art means only Painting. To others it means, perhaps, Painting & Sculpture. We in the West also cloud the issue by adding the idea of Craft to the issue. In Japan, there is no separation of the idea of Art or Craft. Both Art & Craft involve creative processes.

Art can be defined in a number of ways. Firstly it can be defined as human effort to imitate, supplement, alter or counteract the work of nature.

Secondly, Art can be thought of as the conscious production of forms or other elements in a manner that effects the sense of beauty. (Specifically, the production of the beautiful in a graphic or plastic medium.)

Thirdly, Art is a human imaginative skill.

Lastly, Art is a decorative design.

Ikebana aims to improve on the form and style of nature. To create something beautiful and more aesthetically pleasing than is ordinarily experienced in nature.

It can be small, simple and exquisite or massive, bold and very theatrical. It can grace a tiny place, on the table or desk or fill a huge hall, combining light and sound in addition to the mass and form of the flowers and plants that make the spatial composition.

In this book I plan to concentrate on the spatial compositions, using flowers and plants that can be used to beautify and enhance your surroundings in the home. This is truly an Art-Form, and just as paintings and sculpture modify nature and enhance their surroundings, so too will an Ikebana arrangement.

Often as I sit arranging Ikebana, I notice the fresh colour of the leaves, the beauty of Nature, the interesting and different forms and am aware of how relaxing and stress-reducing this ancient art-form is. However, as relaxing as Ikebana is, my interest has been held for twenty years because of the creativity of this art-form.

Once the basic principles have been mastered, the student is encouraged to express freely and creatively, within the confines of the material, the environment and the occasion. The challenge is to use the materials, the flowers and branches, the containers to express your ideas fully within the space available. The seasons of the year and the occasion also influence the materials used. The journey along the Kado, or Road of the Flower, should be a joy for life.

Ikebana is no longer exclusively Japanese or Chinese. It is now taught and practised in over 50 countries of the world. Therefore, it can be said that Ikebana is more popular today than at any time during its long history.

Similarly, other interests have started in many different countries and now have worldwide following. One example of this is the sport of Judo, as seen at the 25th Olympic Games in Barcelona. Many different countries won medals in Judo. As our world becomes smaller because of closer communication ties, we are being influenced by many different cultures. We are truly becoming a "global village".

In Japan, millions of people flock each year to the large Ikebana Exhibitions. Many Exhibitions can be compared with living sculptures and many have modern and creative themes.

There have been few books written in English on Ikebana. Most are now out of print.

In most of the books on Ikebana, the photos have been taken in a studio, with a plain background! We do not live our lives with a plain background. One of the reasons for this is that Japanese homes are, in the main, small. Another reason is that Ikebana has only developed worldwide since the end of the Second World War. There is a strong worldwide interest in seeing Ikebana used in the home. Australian Ikebana is of interest to people of other countries, just as we find the art of other countries interesting. The trees, shrubs and flowers bring a distinctly Australian style, combined with our climate and style of living. Our homes and gardens are, on average, much bigger than the homes in Japan. Even though homes are on average smaller in Japan, many Ikebana arrangements are so large as to cover a whole theatre stage. I have even seen Ikebana in a lift in Tokyo and have often seen Ikebana in Police Stations and other unusual places. However, as I feel most people learn Ikebana to improve their home and I have never seen a book which focuses on Ikebana in the home, I'm sure you will enjoy this book.

The homes in which I have completed the Ikebana are all beautiful and exemplify the best of Australian Style. I wanted to show Ikebana enthusiasts all over the world the best of Australian style. However, even the smallest space will be improved with an arrangement. The Japanese are masters at making the smallest space beautiful. In Japan, I am often surprised and delighted, after walking through many built-up areas, to come across a beautiful miniature garden or an unexpected Ikebana arrangement.

Contrasts are very much a part of this Art-form. The positive and the negative play an important role.

It is important to develop your own individual style. This doesn't come without study. It is said it takes three years to master the basics of Ikebana. When you have mastered the basic rules of design and form you should be able to communicate your own feelings and purpose of the arrangement to the person viewing it. Some of these feelings could be – happiness, celebration, drama, elegance, modernity, naturalness, peacefulness, loudness and quietness.

All of these are part of Ikebana, a part of our world.

INTRODUCTION

Is it really necessary to have everything "just so"?

When you feel there are a dozen things you have to do before you can relax, it may be time to take a cue from the principles of Ikebana, which suggest that it isn't necessary or even desirable to have everything in perfect order.

The whole concept of perfection as we think of it doesn't exist in the Buddhist mind. Zen Buddhists see symmetry (the Western ideal of perfection) as being fatal to the imagination and fatal to individual experience. When something is asymmetrical, you have to involve the self – you have to complete the picture in your own mind!

Sometimes it may be more interesting to leave things as they are, and appreciate the potential in something incomplete or look at it in a new way, rather than finish it right now.

Nature grows in an asymmetrical way.

The word Ikebana means "living flowers" or "bringing flowers to life".

The Japanese have a saying, that if we take the life of a flower, we have an obligation to make it look more beautiful.

Ikebana is a Philosophy, its essence is a way of life. Our attitude is based upon a way of looking at and living with Nature. Nature may be used, but is not exploited.

In some European garden designs, for example, Man's hand is the dominating feature. One of the principles of Japanese garden design and Ikebana is that Man plays a small part in the overall design. Heaven, Earth and Man combine together to make an asymmetrical triangle.

Heaven is the most important element, Earth, the second most important element, and Man – the smallest part of the asymmetrical triangle – but also the most beautiful.

Not until after World War II was it possible to learn Ikebana. In the past men have dominated. Buddhist monks, Samurai warriors and male teachers controlled the knowledge for hundreds of years. Many men still learn Ikebana. I have been told that many retired Japanese executives learn Ikebana, because they have the time for this hobby.

They enjoy learning Ikebana because it is very relaxing and because of their great love of Nature. Many of the big schools of Ikebana in Japan still have men as headmasters. One of the main reasons for this is the hereditary nature underlying the ownership of these schools. They are passed from father to son or daughter, whichever the case may be. The major schools are well-established, wealthy and influential. Women now form the largest group who learn Ikebana. Women are considered more feminine if they learn flower arranging.

We have always been interested in making our homes and living environment more attractive. Even in Ancient Egypt, the remains of flowers in vases have been found.

Why has Ikebana grown in popularity in the West? Why has it spread to so many countries and appeals to so many differing types of people?

Obviously, the Ikebana in Africa, U.S.A., South America, India, U.K., Europe, Australia and the over fifty countries worldwide will all vary in style – because of the different climates and different flowers, shrubs and trees, and also because of the differing life-styles of the different countries.

IKEBANA INTERNATIONAL has been responsible for the spread and growing popularity of Ikebana. Ikebana International, or I.I. as it is known, is a worldwide organisation which was founded in Tokyo, Japan, in 1956, by an

American General's wife, Ellen Gordon Allen. I.I. is a non-profit, cultural organisation.The motto of I.I. is "Friendship Through Flowers". Over the many years I have been a member of I.I. I have met interesting, positive and creative people from different countries and from different walks of life.

Whenever there is an I.I. Conference, it's as if the word goes forth worldwide, and people gather in a non-competitive, friendly way.

The Australia/New Zealand Region of I.I. has 13 Chapters (or Clubs) within the Region. The Melbourne Chapter of I.I. was the first Chapter in Australia and is over 30 years old. The Gold Coast Chapter was formed in 1988. I had the honour of being the Founding President of the Gold Coast Chapter. I.I. is a uniting organisation which brings all peoples, of all ages, together in an appreciation of beauty.

Many of the students at my Ikebana centre, come from other countries – as well as Australian-born and New Zealand-born students. New Guinea is also close to Australia, and many New Guineans, now live here. Many people from New Caledonia, Vanuatu and the other Pacific Islands live here too; as well as those with a European, Asian and other backgrounds. The Japanese population has also increased over the past five years. We have an interesting mix!

In a world where stress levels seem to be increasing, our heart rate can be lowered and blood pressure lowered by practising Ikebana. The involvement with Ikebana is good for you physically, mentally, socially and spiritually.

Another reason Ikebana has grown so much in popularity in the West (besides its comparatively recent introduction) is that there is a basic economy of materials used. We no longer have the money to spend on enormous amounts of flowers. We don't have large flower gardens. The Conservation Movement has influenced everyone to conserve and protect our environment for the future.

Architects are becoming more aware of the importance of incorporating Nature into their designs. Environmental Architecture is becoming more important. We do not like to be dehumanised by sterile spaces.

I always have Ikebana in my home and find it adds a happy, interesting, and "live" Art-form to the home. I hope you enjoy this book and are able to use or adapt some of the ideas to make them your own.

Before beginning the book, I would like to share with you the reasons for choosing each of The Homes, The Gold Coast Art Gallery, The Sheraton-Mirage Hotel (Gold Coast) and the Royal Pines Hotel (A Prince Hotel – Gold Coast) – Display Homes.

When you look at each of the homes you will notice the different backgrounds, settings, environments. The style of homes are very different. Arranging Ikebana in the home has always been a challenge. The arrangement must fit into the space available. It must fit in with the theme and mood we want to impart. Before starting the book I gave considerable thought to a number of things. These were – the type of home, the area in which the Ikebana was to be placed, the container to be used, the materials available, the owners of the home, and their lifestyle and I sketched many designs.

There were 12 locations.

1. Family Home. I chose this home because it is a Classic. It will not become dated or old-fashioned quickly and is casually elegant. It has a Mediterranean style which suits the Gold Coast's climate and lifestyle. It was wonderful to be able to use the beautiful garden as a background too.

2. Island Living. This superb home is situated on its own private island. Each room has wonderful views and yet it remains a comfortable family home. The home was very well designed for the tropical climate, with large spaces for light and air. The Ikebana arrangements have a colourful, tropical and happy feeling.

3. The Waterfront Home. This elegant home features soft grey and has a quiet atmosphere. Water is featured by the use of large windows in the home. Water also plays an important role in the lives of the owners. I featured the use of water and the reflections.

4. The Penthouse. The Penthouse is spectacular and dramatic. The owners have happily and effectively adapted the Asian influence into this strongly European home. It was wonderful to create Ikebana here.

5. The New Guinea Influence. This home is interesting as the owners have an outstanding collection of New Guinea native artifacts.The rustic and ethnic feeling of the artifacts provides an interesting contrast to the Scandinavian influence in the house design. Original and creative Ikebana was possible, using the New Guinea artifacts.

6. The Gold Coast City Art Gallery. The Art Gallery embodies the feeling of Art. It demonstrated that even in an area highlighting Art, Ikebana lifted and added a magical touch to the Gallery. The paintings were definitely enhanced by the arrangements and features on the paintings were brought out by the Ikebana.

7. Modern Home. This home is a modern, stylish home. It is very suited to modern Ikebana.

8. The Sheraton-Mirage Hotel (Gold Coast). I chose this Hotel, from the many available, because I admire its architecture and style very much.

9. The Royal Pines Hotel (A Prince Hotel – Gold Coast) – Display Homes.

These smart and stylish homes had just been opened to the public. The fact that they were brand new and demonstrated a lot of the current style of living on the Gold Coast was a strong reason to choose them. Their wonderful aspect onto the lake and golf course also made them very appealing. These homes have a high level of security and I felt that their sophisticated design would be enhanced with Ikebana.

10. Mansion. This out of the ordinary home has been built in the grand style. Huge spaces and lofty ceilings presented a challenge with space. The arrangement in the entrance had to fit in with the large space, without appearing too massive.

It had to provide gracious elegance and refinement.

11. Farm Cottage. This lovely little cottage shows a different aspect of the Gold Coast and shows a different aspect of Ikebana. I do not think that the "country cottage" style of flower-arranging must always go with country environments. The modern, stylish arrangements I have created match well with the outdoors, the mountain scenery and the farm.

12. The Home with views. Glorious views of the Gold Coast must daily delight the owners of this home. A luxuriant, tropical Ikebana complemented the spectacular scenery.

FAMILY HOME

The first Ikebana arrangement appears in the bedroom. The size of the space must be considered. The intimacy is enhanced by this simple, elegant arrangement. The moon container wishes the viewer good fortune, whilst the white Gardenias gently perfume the air in this summer arrangement.

Container: A black wooden moon.

Materials: Gardenia, fern, black and gold and black and silver tiny balls on black wire. The wire has been bent to follow the curve of the moon container. The arrangement is contained within the moon shape. In Ikebana the space created is as important as the arrangement created. The space defines the shape. The reflection in the mirror increases the beauty.

"Glimpsed through a crevice in the garden fence,
one white flower is spring's impermanence."
A Haiku poem by Buson.

Water is necessary for life. This simple truth is so taken for granted that we can easily overlook the cultural significance of water. But if we explore the function of water more deeply, we find that in cultures throughout the world water has strong religious connotations. In Japan, the idea that water removes the contamination of mind and body is especially strong. Ikebana looks striking in this garden. The sun glints on the red wire and the wind gently moves the wires, casting gleaming rays of light in this arrangement. The water of the fountain and pond is an important backdrop to the arrangement.

Container: Grey ceramic, with a gold feature.

Materials: Red Celosia and red wire.

"How visibly the gentle morning airs
Stir in the caterpillar's hairs!"
A Haiku poem by Buson.

Running water is often associated with time. We only have so much allotted time in our life. We must make the most of our time available.
Colour plays an important role on this hot summer's day. The white daisies and the bleached mulberry branch echo the cool feeling of the water. The sound of the gentle fountain reminds us of the sound of a clear, cool stream. The hand-made white, glass container complements the cool colour-scheme.

Container: White glass.

Materials: A branch of bleached Mulberry, Daisies, German Statice or Limonium.

Summer. "What burning stillness! Brass cicada-drones
Drill their resonance into rocks and stones."
A Haiku poem by Basho.

The Peony in the East is the symbol of financial success and success in general.
In the West it is known as "The King of the Flowers". It is certainly very happy when arranged in a glamorous way.
The dining-room setting is formal and elegant. The Ikebana adds a richness and glamour to the room.

Container: Pink and mauve ceramic container.

Materials: Peony, Gypsophila, pink glitter flares, naturally curling water-reeds.

"Happiness is like a butterfly.
The more you chase it, the more it will elude you, but if you turn your attention to other things it will come and softly sit on your shoulder." Anon.

The Phalaenopsis Orchid is commonly called the Butterfly Orchid and has pride of place in this arrangement. This is a celebratory arrangement, a Christmas arrangement. Red is the colour of celebration. Ikebana is fun, especially when it can be shared with family and friends! A warm, friendly welcome is given to everyone. The open fan is a symbol of welcome and this shape has been echoed in the red wire.

Container: An interesting, twisted red ceramic container.

Materials: Mangrove root, Dracena Marginata, Phalaenopsis orchids and red wire.

Even the smallest arrangement has charm and attracts the eye. The emphasis of this arrangement is on the one beautiful flower, the Rose ("Fragrant Plum" – which is described in the Rose Catalogue as Plum-Purple with an all-pervading scent). Johann Goethe described "The ideal of beauty is simplicity and tranquillity."

Container: A hand-made glass container.

Materials: "Fragrant Plum" Rose, Statice and blue wire.

The entrance of the home is an important area, because this is the area that welcomes and creates the impression of the rest of the home. This arrangement is a summer arrangement. It is happy and tropical in feeling. The aim was to combine fresh and unconventional material.

Container: A hand-made glass container.

Materials: Massed Bougainvillea, Dipladenia (creeper) – "Scarlet Pimpernel" and silver and gold metallic, holed ribbon.

Line and Mass are important elements in Ikebana. Balance, Harmony and Design must be considered too.
In this arrangement, the black metal container contrasts well against the white shutters. The balance of the line and mass is in harmony with the container and the space.

Container: A black metal container.
Materials: Twisted Willow, Azalea and Phalaenopsis Orchid.

Music, Art and Ikebana have many things in common.
"Flowers . . . have a mysterious and subtle influence upon the feelings, not unlike some strains of music. They relax the tenseness of the mind. They dissolve its rigour."
Henry Ward Beecher, "Eyes and Ears".

The shape of this container is indicative of Music and Metronomes.
The blue and mauve of the Hydrangea combines well with the modern use of the purple wire. The wire brings to mind piano-wires in this situation.

Container: A triangular, black ceramic container.

Materials: Hydrangea and purple wire.

The beauty of the light and reflections, together with the yellow colour, give the impression of a sunny day. Yellow-Gold is a lucky colour in Ikebana and is the National Colour of Australia – The Green and Gold of Australia.
Kenzans or needlepoint holders were not used in this arrangement. These would detract from the beauty of the clean, clear water and sparkling crystal. The Ikebana had to be viewed from all angles. The interest was centred on the unusual and beautiful Golden Calla Lily. This is also an area of the home where we meet and talk with visiting friends. Like a friendly embrace or the warm shaking of hands, the flowers stretch to meet each other from different containers.

Container: Two crystal glass containers.

Material: Golden Calla Lily – "Zantedeschia".

As Australians, water plays an integral part in our lives. The popularity of the family pool testifies to our need to surround ourselves with water. In the midst of a scorchingly hot summer's day I designed this container, which could bring water into the home. I wanted to be able to use water in an unexpected and modern way and still convey its refreshing coolness. The soft material used contrasted against the strong horizontal lines of the shutters. The Australian Native, Banksia, was featured in the water and within the cloud of Gypsophila. The Gypsophila was used in a cloud-like way.

Container: A red, black and clear perspex container.

Material: Gypsophila, Banksia.

Australia has developed into a Multicultural Nation over the past thirty years. The Cultural influences are often freshly Australian and come from a number of different countries. This grouping of objects reflects this International-mix which has become part of Australia.

Even the smallest arrangement harmonises with its environment.

In this Ikebana texture is important. The texture of the German Statice adds dimension and interest to the space. The vivid red of the Celosia has been muted by the German Statice and has been used as a colour accent. The container is an interesting one.

Container: A ceramic container.

Materials: German Statice, Red Celosia, Kiwi Vine.

ISLAND LIVING

I think the Golden Shower Tree is the most beautiful tree. It flowers in Summer in Australia (around Christmas and New Year) and Australia is the country of Summer! Yellow is the colour of joy! The container is understated. The beautiful golden flowers are the focus of the arrangement. The Palm branches have a supporting role in the design and the golden ribbon added an extra subtle richness. This large, delicate arrangement complemented the large Entrance area, added a vitality to the space and created a vibrant atmosphere, which reflected the busy life of the family.

Container: A tall, clear glass container.

Materials: The Golden Shower Tree, Palm, gold ribbon.

The Golden Shower has been used in a different way. In this smaller arrangement, just one branch has been used. The beautiful flowers are still important to the design of the Ikebana. There is an understanding that the flowers will fall, that life continues through the four seasons & life renews itself. Even though we go through hard times, these do not last. This is a classical Ikebana arrangement, adapted to a modern environment. The softness is reflected in the soft Asparagus fern. The summer feeling in the Iris straps.
A wonderful thing to look at while having a cup of tea or coffee!

Container: Ceramic container.
Materials: Golden Shower/Golden Cassia/Rainbow Shower, Iris, Asparagus fern.

Trusting the wind –
"Simply have faith: let all attachments go.
Do not blossoms scatter, even so?" –
A Haiku poem by Issa.

The rich deep colours of the Cornus Dogwood provided a vivid splash of colour to the Dining-room. The fresh, bright feeling suited this elegant but casual occasion. The umbrella grass added interest but didn't block the view of the guests. The Ikebana could be viewed from all around, it didn't contain a specific front or back. A feeling of lightness was achieved by not massing the flowers too tightly. The beautiful colour in the glass complemented the flower colour and was echoed in various elements in the room. A harmonious, colourful and interesting arrangement was the result.

Container: A hand-made glass container.

Materials: Umbrella Grass, Cornus Dogwood.

Even though Ikebana is an Art, it can live with you in the most common spaces. Isn't this a wonderful Kitchen! When traditional English bunched flowers are contrasted with Ikebana, we notice how creative Ikebana is. Always different, there is never a sameness about it. In this Ikebana, the curved container served as a contrast to the many straight lines in the kitchen. The soft green colour of the container harmonised well with the fresh, white Chrysanthemums. The Umbrella Grass stems extended the space and served as a design element. The dried grass heads had been sprayed silver. The grass added texture and interest. Space was left in the container, in order to give a feeling of freedom and unrestricted space to the viewer.

Container: A ceramic container.

Materials: Chrysanthemums, dried grass heads, Umbrella Grass stems.

Ikebana makes us look closely at everything growing around us. Not only flowers, but tree shapes, leaf shapes, textures and curves. In this Ikebana, the curve of the Cactus leaf is strong and interesting. The Cactus combined well with the Banksia, because the Banksia is such a unique and strong flower. The container was used in a supportive way. It is an interesting container, because of its unusual shape and glaze. Even though the materials used are strong, the Ikebana is not overpowering because the colours are not dominant. The lines on the table-top draw our gaze to the Ikebana and our interest is held because of the strength of the design and the unusual material.

Container: A ceramic container.

Materials: Cactus leaf, Banksia.

THE WATERFRONT HOME

Water plays an important part in the lives of the owners of this home.

They have a great love of sailing. The owners show this by their choice of greys and blues and their large picture windows. I emphasised this love of water and brought water into their home in a dramatic way, by using a large, transparent blue orb. I felt this would be a more sophisticated approach than adding extravagant colour or other discordant elements in this situation.

It was natural to have an arrangement that featured water, and reflections in the water. The crisp colour of the New Zealand Flax and the fresh Rose, combined with the reflecting light, strengthened the transparent beauty of the water. The Australian Blue Gum on the left and the skyline of Surfers Paradise can be seen in the background. This large orb is the outstanding feature of this room. Our eye is drawn to it and it holds our interest in a dramatic way.

Container: Blue glass container.

Materials: New Zealand Flax, Rose("Papageno")

This arrangement was completed in the late afternoon. It captured the delicate glow of the afternoon light, at sunset. The overall feeling is one of quietness and coolness, after the heat of a summer's day.

"Sea Holly", Statice and Mirrored Steel was my choice, because of their "cool" colours. The flowers used added a soft, quiet touch only.

Container: Blue ceramic container.

Materials: Sea Holly, Statice, Creeper "Bower of Beauty" – Pandorea Jasminoides, Mirrored Steel.

THE PENTHOUSE

The "seishin" or "spirit" of this Ikebana is modern, dramatic, colourful and celebratory. The red doors set the scene and an arrangement can be seen through the doors. The black metal container and stand give the feeling of the ultra-modern. The lines of the container and stand provide a contrast to the vertical and horizontal lines already present. The Gypsophila has been sprayed red. The broom bristles have been sprayed red, white and black. The feeling is one of a dramatic entrance into a beautiful, elegant world.

Container: A black metal container and stand.

Materials: Gypsophila, broom bristles and red Celosia.

This arrangement is also dramatic. The beautiful large glass container looks like a giant pearl that has been washed up out of the ocean, which is in the background. The King Protea looks stylish and its circular shape matches well with the circular shape of the container. The Kiwi Vine has been used to extend the Ikebana and adds space to the composition. The feeling is one of beauty and drama.

Container: Hand-made glass container.

Materials: Kiwi Vine, King Protea, Statice, Gypsophila and Pussy Willow.

There is a vital difference between "▼" and "▲". The container shape is reflected in the light shape. The design is a modern, sculptural one. The interesting material intrigues the viewer.

Container: A ceramic container, with painted accent.

Materials: Hydrangea, Palm Seed + Pods, Monstera leaf and Statice.

This Ikebana arrangement is featured in an Alcove or "Tokonoma".
Just a very brief amount of historical information is necessary to explain the alcove. In the 15th Century we see Ikebana used as an Art and not as part of a religion. From 1400 to 1568 there are pictures, still preserved, of Ikebana used in alcoves or Tokonoma. At this time, there are also records of flower parties e.g. Cherry-Blossom Viewing Parties. The Japanese valued Ikebana so highly that the basic design of their home was altered to incorporate an alcove, or area, for viewing their Ikebana. Japanese Architecture preserved the alcove until comparatively modern times. In the new apartments and houses, alcoves are not usually present, because of lack of space and the influence of the West on living conditions, since the War.
Here in this lovely penthouse, there is a modern alcove. The arrangement I have completed, to fit in the modern alcove, is an arrangement from the classical school of Ikebana, the Ikenobo School. The style of arrangement is called a Shimputai arrangement.
"A flower is utterly beautiful when filled by the feeling of life". Anon.
The dramatic effect is achieved by featuring only one flower, in a large space. The eye is caught and held by the Rose. This Ikebana is elegant because of its ultimate simplicity.

Container: A ceramic container, with a gold feature.

Materials: Weeping Willow, Rose ("Mon Cheri") and Fairy Statice.

I introduced the circular shape into this area that already contained many straight lines. The importance of the circle can be seen in the stepping-stones, the holes in the Ikebana container and in the circular flowers (The Proteas and the Waterlilies.) The arrangement has a casual elegance, which contrasts well with the more rigid lines in the background.
The feeling of this Ikebana is dramatic and opulent. The sun glints on the waterlilies in the pond and the wind blows gently across the water. The whole scene refreshes the spirit. This modern Ikebana added a creative and free feeling. The modern container is unusual. I have used the Dodder Vine in a free way, so that the beauty of the three King Proteas was emphasised.
Many rules govern Ikebana. One such rule is that the number three is lucky, whereas four is not advised! The Japanese word for "four", shi, is homonymous with that for "death".
In Ikebana, the emphasis is on the beauty of life.

Container: Creative ceramic container.

Materials: Dodder vine and King Proteas.

Ikebana comes from the heart. It is not a matter of putting bunches of flowers in vases. It is important in Ikebana to involve yourself in the whole composition. Therefore the flower-arrangement is always dynamic, interesting and creative.
Water is featured in this arrangement. The iridescent paper emphasises the water. A rainbow effect is created by the rays of the setting sun striking the water and the iridescent paper in the late afternoon. The trimmed spear-grass appears clean-cut and dynamic. The lily added a point of interest to the arrangement.

Container: Three round, clear glass containers.

Material: Iridescent paper, Spear grass, Lily.

THE NEW GUINEA INFLUENCE

The home-owners of this home lived for many years in New Guinea. They have a fascinating collection of tribal artefacts.Their home best suits Ikebana that incorporates and uses this interest. The flower-arrangements have been influenced by the primitive art of the wild New Guinea tribesmen, compared with the previous home, which was influenced by Asia and Europe, and especially Japan. The Ikebana reflects the New Guinea interest. The colours, in the main, are earthy and the textures and designs interesting.

The stories are fascinating surrounding the New Guinea objects, and I have included them too! The grass skirt and the New Guinea head are connected with a MOKA, a very important occurrence in Highland New Guinea life.

As the story goes . . .

"One misty morning, with the dew still on the ground, a man emerged from the pit pit (tall bamboo grass) and stealthily approached a herd of pigs foraging in the mud for edible roots and worms. He seized the largest pig and placing it across his shoulders, as quickly as his burden would allow, ran off in the direction of his own land and safety. Another man hunting in nearby bush saw a quick movement on the track. Surprised he investigated and found extra deep footprints in the mud and suspiciously gave chase. As his quarry came in sight he realised the man was from a neighbouring clan. With all his strength he hurled his spear, transfixing the thief through his lower back. The thief stumbled and the pig slid down his back to be supported by the shaft of the protruding spear. Realising he was going to die he bravely continued back to his own house to die an honourable death rather than be axed by the enemy.

In November 1983, in the Nebilyer Valley, thirteen kilometres from Mount Hagen, a Moka took place. The Moka is a traditional ceremonial exchange of wealth. It is said to date back hundreds of years. The Moka system is extremely complex and is generally based on compensation for deaths and injuries incurred, and rewards for allegiances during tribal conflicts. This compensation is not usually a singular payment, but forms part of a cycle that is often carried through succeeding generations. The men and women oiled their bodies, painted their faces and had splendid headdresses.Finally the wealth was officially distributed. A whole generation had passed since the death of the pig thief, and the sons had fulfilled the obligation of their parents."

Part of a story told by Roey Berger and Neil Ryan, Curators of the Western Highlands Cultural Gallery in Mount Hagen.

In this kitchen-table Ikebana I have used a New Guinea grass skirt in an unusual way. The colour and texture of the skirt, within the container, bring out the texture, colour and glaze of the container. The New Guinea head adds interest. The Hibiscus adds a tropical accent and reminds us of the heat and tropical location of New Guinea.

Container: A ceramic container.

Materials: Grass skirt, Hibiscus, New Guinea Head.

I have used a Bilum in this Ikebana, because the Bilum is such an important part of New Guinea life.

As Maureen Mackenzie, from the Institute of Papua New Guinea Studies, said . . . "The Bilum is a net bag . . . an essential accessory of everyday life in Papua New Guinea. Used by man, woman and child, they are evident everywhere. They come in all shapes and sizes. They display an overwhelming variety of strong and vital designs. They are one of the most useful objects in the country; and, more than this, they reflect the flavour of society and social values at large today. The art of bilum-making allows for new forms of creative expression, which are relevant to the changing times – it is a true contemporary folk art. New Guinea life can be seen to be contained by the bilum, as life begins in one (used as a baby's cradle) and ends in one (in death the spirit is invited to return to the bilum of the mourner) and life is nourished by one (by food stored and carried in the bilum)".

The aim of my Ikebana was therefore to show off this interesting cloth bag. The bilum is the focal point of the arrangement. The New Guinea native seems to be looking over the arrangement. The container is a modern copy of an Ikebana container hundreds of years old. The "ancient" mood of the container suits the mood of the area in which it has been placed. The bright colours of the cloth catch the eye. The colour and texture of the Alliums add a natural and interesting texture and the colour is not dominant or eye-catching. The Allium is used in a secondary way to the bilum. The circular Allium reflect the circle of life of the New Guinea cloth bag.

Container: A ceramic container.

Materials: Alliums, New Guinea Hand-made material bag – The Bilum.

The spears are a feature of this Ikebana. They were made by the Biamis in a very remote part of Papua, New Guinea, on the Nomad River on the edge of the Great Papuan Plateau, 300 kilometres north-north-west of Daru in the Western Province and only 120 metres above sea level.

Unlike most villagers in Papua New Guinea, the Biamis live all together in one, sometimes two, large communal houses. Built in clearings in heavy rainforest, the houses can be as much as 20 metres wide and 50 or so metres long.

The usual plan of the Biamis house includes first, immediately behind the front door, a communal room. It is used as a kitchen, a store for food and water, dining, meetings and entertainment. Behind this is a raised central pavilion which is the sleeping quarters for the men. It is well protected by a long room on each side. (One side for women, the other side for pigs.) The back section of their common long house is a clubhouse for the men. The arrows and spears made by the male Biamis are some of the most intricately carved spears in New Guinea. The spears are used for hunting and fishing.

The ceramic container is entitled "Tornado", which conjures up a feeling of storms, the ocean and fishing. The spears are used for fishing and the owner's boat is sitting outside – just waiting to go fishing! The weeping, brown gum has been used to balance the arrangement, adds a harmonious colour and a different texture. The lines of the spears provide a dynamic extension to the container. The bright red Anthuriums added an asymmetrical focal point. The lines on the boat outside the window have been brought into the design. The outside has been brought inside and been incorporated into the whole.

Container: A ceramic container.

Materials: New Guinea Spears, Weeping Gum, Anthurium.

In this arrangement two containers have been used. The containers are entitled "fish" and are modern representations of fish. The shape made by fish swimming through the water. The black and white containers provide contrast – the positive and the negative – and similarity of shape. The Tortured Willow has been used in a free way, in order to free the arrangement from the bold base of the containers. The Chrysanthemum used is a fresh, happy colour and appears like water-spray off the backs of the fish. The feeling is a natural, happy one which is reflected in the mirror.

Container: A black and white ceramic container.

Materials: Chrysanthemum, Tortured Willow.

I have converted a prized piece into a container by using imagination. This little hand-woven pig adds a touch of fun!

Container: Woven New Guinea Pig.
Material: Tortured Willow, Banksia.

The beautiful colours in this arrangement bring to mind the exotic plumage of the New Guinea Native worn on ceremonial occasions. The sharpness of the lines of the home is contrasted with the softness of the curtain fabric and the soft textures of the wood. Colour plays an important role in this Ikebana. Some of the materials used are "native" materials e.g. Spear Grass, and are wild. The effect is not sophisticated or dramatic, such as those used in the Penthouse. The effect is exotic and colourful.

Container: A hand-made glass container.
Materials: Coloured Kiwi Vine, Spear Grass, Statice, Cornflower and Allium.

THE GOLD COAST CITY ART GALLERY

All of the Ikebana arrangements in the Art Gallery have a modern and dramatic feeling. Even though Sculpture has been used, the compositions still remain Ikebana. Recently, there was a Henry Moore Exhibition of Sculpture, in the Art Gallery. Henry Moore described, in a video, how he used the same shapes over and over again in the creative process, until he achieved the composition he wanted. We can see a merging of the creative process in Art, Ikebana and Sculpture. It is always interesting in Ikebana to give exactly the same material to a group of Ikebana students. The same material will change to suit the environment and change to suit the individual!

When I first arrived at the Art Gallery, one of the Art Gallery Volunteers had arranged a "Wedding-type" of flower-arrangement using drooping white lilies. When this was dismantled and Ikebana in place, the whole Art Gallery looked more modern, more smart and more like an Art Gallery. It is important to think about the area where the Ikebana is to be placed. The mood and atmosphere can be changed dramatically by adding appropriate Ikebana.

The black metal sculptured container is modern. The triangular shapes in the container stand are echoed in the painting behind. The red Gypsophila is a dramatic splash of colour, complementing the painting and the area in which it has been placed. The white area on the painting becomes a more interesting feature. The features in the painting stand out more, such as the red lines.

Container: A black iron container, on a metal stand.

Materials: Gypsophila.

The strong, dramatic line of the sculpture emphasises the fragility of the material used – the King Protea and the Statice. (Man-made V's natural material.) I designed and made the Sculpture. The curved lines of the metal sculpture fit into the larger space well. The large painting on the left has a similar upward curve in it. The King Protea is a long-lasting flower, as is the Statice. If we are living with flowers, we are happy if we do not have to replace them too often.

Container: Sculpture.

Materials: King Protea, Statice.

The Australian Black-Boy is a native plant, which grows in the wild, bush areas of Australia. Aboriginal people would relate immediately to this tough, striking and impressive plant. In this Ikebana I placed the emphasis on the Black-Boy. The top of the plant imitates the design of the Aboriginal painting on the left. The desert landscape atmosphere of the painting is enhanced because of the use of the Black-Boy. The use of the paler pink Anthurium has been used in a supportive way, because the eye must be drawn to the Black-Boy. The beautiful glass container has been used to add a modern feeling, as has the white plastic material.

Container: A white hand-made glass container.

Materials: Black-Boy, Anthurium, white plastic material.

Kathleen WHISKY
Australia/NT
Two Travelling Women 1985
Acrylic on canvas
149.0 x 100.5cm
Purchased 1985 by the Gold Coast Art Acquisition Society
KATHLEEN WHISKY
TWO TRAVELLING WOMEN

I chose this material because it is fresh and new. The Air-Conditioning pipe was left-over from air-conditioning my office.

It is an innovative idea, and adds a modern, interesting and fresh look to the corner of the Art Gallery. The Spear Grass gave a sense of vertical movement to the arrangement. The Christmas Lilies added colour and with the Asparagus Fern supported this modern design. The corner of the Art Gallery was vitalised by having this interesting arrangement in this space.

Container: Air-conditioning pipe.

Materials: Spear Grass, Christmas Lilies, Asparagus Fern.

THE MODERN HOME

Ikebana has the power to enhance the basic theme of the Architect, Builder, Interior Designer and Owner, as well as adding an interesting focal point and bringing Living Material into the home.
This home could best be described as fresh, up to date and modern. The Ikebana containers I chose were beautiful hand-made glass containers with a very modern feeling. The gold and green bronze container in the Lounge Room has an elegant shape and is decorative, as is the gold lacquered tray. The materials used were all exotic, tropical plants, which had a modern appearance. I did not choose old-fashioned material or fussy material. The home has clean lines, space and has a fresh feeling. The Ikebana complemented this fresh and modern feeling.

The vibrant, golden Tiger Lilies wish the viewer good fortune. Yellow is the colour that symbolises joy and good fortune. I bought this beautiful bronze container in a tiny little back street in Kyoto, Japan. I have now owned it for 20 years and still enjoy using it and enjoy its colour and shape and texture. The Japanese and other Ikebana enthusiasts all over the world own many vases. These are usually packed away and brought out for the relevant season of the year or for special occasions. All vases owned are not displayed all the time.
When they are unpacked they still have a freshness, and we have not grown tired of them by having them on view all through the year. I sometimes wonder where the Japanese store their Ikebana containers!
The bamboo container has been placed on its side to add interest to the composition. The gold wire was used to unite the bronze and bamboo and gold lacquered tray into one cohesive whole. The pine wishes long life to all. The clean water in the tray is also part of the Ikebana and adds a feeling of coolness and reflective elegance to the arrangement. The Ikebana connects the sides of the table together and therefore brings people together.

Container: A bronze container, a small celadon container, a bamboo container and a gold lacquered tray.

Materials: Tiger Lilies, Gold wire and pine.

The colour pink is most important in this room. I chose the pink Oriental Lily for this area because of its pink colour and large size. It also has a beautiful perfume and this is important to us too! We could sit and listen to music or watch T.V. and enjoy the beauty and perfume of the Ikebana. The modern, clean-cut container has a splash of pink on it. I added the pink twists to the branches of the Oleander in order to see the interesting lines and pink colour. The branches were used as line in the arrangement and the pink Oriental Lily was used as mass.

Container: Hand-made glass container.

Materials: Oriental Lily, dried Oleander branch, pink twists.

This Ikebana is feminine and adds Romance to everyday, functional furniture. The arrangement connects the sides of the table together – just as it does in the Lounge Room – thus bringing people together.
The modern, fresh feeling gives an up-to-date feeling to the table. The mini-roses soften and add splashes of colour. The candle adds Romance!

Container: A hand-made glass container.
Materials: New Zealand Flax, Mini-Roses (Magic Carousel) and Candle.

In this area music is important. The stereo is nearby, and so it was natural that my Ikebana was influenced by music. The silver wire reminds us of Guitar wires. The arrangement still has a modern, fresh, up-to-date theme, which was continued into this area. This uncommon glass container is enhanced by the modern use of the silver wire. The Ikebana stands out from the background. The single red Gebera is pivotal to the arrangement.

Container: Hand-made glass container. Clear glass with a dribbled black line.

Materials: Silver wire, Lotus Pods and Gerbera.

Exotic materials have been used in modern containers in this home. When we contrast this home with, say, the New Guinea Influence home, where not so exotic flowers and materials were used with exotic containers and New Guinea artefacts, we notice the difference. I have placed the emphasis on the exotic materials in this arrangement.
Mangrove trees can be seen growing on the island opposite the home. So, I have brought the distance into the Ikebana by using this interesting Mangrove root. This arrangement has been designed to be seen from all angles, especially while cooking in the Kitchen! The owner of this home catches delicious fish and crabs often, and is an excellent cook. The Crab Claw and Heliconia add a graphic, fresh, modern feeling. The Heliconia repeat the shape of the glass container. The whole theme is one of new, innovative design.

Container: A hand-made glass container, much like the shape of Australia.

Materials: Mangrove Root, Crab Claw, Heliconia and Statice.

THE SHERATON MIRAGE HOTEL

The sound of the thundering waterfall echoes through the Entrance. The Hotel is surrounded by water. The Pacific Ocean lies to the East, the Nerang River to the West. Within the grounds of the Mirage are many fountains and ponds, as well as the swimming pool areas.

As I was completing the arrangement, a family of black swans zoomed in for a jet-style landing . . . with landing-gear feet at the ready!
So water, the sound of water and reflections in water feature in this Hotel. The theme of the Ikebana echoed this theme. The plastic rods added a glistening, shimmering, water-like appearance to the arrangement on this Summer's day. The water flowing in the fountain in the background became an echo. The container is modern and the shape of the top of the container matched the top of the fountain well. Water can be seen through the hole in the centre and becomes part of the whole composition. The flowers, Crepe Myrtle, incorporated the gentle breeze and a feeling of airyness and coolness was able to be achieved. The Weeping Willow added line to the plastic rods and gave an added feeling of a water-plant to the Ikebana.

> "A black swan swimming to the shore beyond
> Parts with his breast the flower-petalled pond."

Container: A free-style ceramic container.

Materials: Crepe Myrtle (Lagerstroemia) – white and pink, Weeping Willow and plastic rods.

THE ROYAL PINES HOTEL

The newly opened homes had been built close to the Hotel and Golf Course. Security is a feature of the homes and they have up-to-the-minute style.
I felt that Ikebana would enhance their style.

This is an Ikebana arrangement for busy people. It is simple and easy to do. The clean glass container has been filled with sea shells. You could easily have fun collecting the shells, too. The sea shells have been used as a kenzan or support. The Spear Grass has been placed into the shells. The vertical shape adds a dynamic feeling. The yellow roses are not the centre of interest. They have been used in a secondary way, to support and add to the Ikebana. The shells, slightly magnified in the water, are the focal point of the arrangement. Our eye is drawn to the interesting Ikebana, where the emphasis has been placed on water, while in the background, through the window, we see water and the golf-course.

Container: A large, round, glass cylinder, filled with sea-shells.

Materials: Spear Grass and Roses (Holtermann's Gold).

LEGENDS

Again, the approach is more simple, for the active person (Golfer) or Home Entertainer. It reflects that the busy person still has time for beauty and Nature, even with a busy lifestyle.

This is a soft, clean, crisp arrangement. The plastic rods have been bent into circles to match the circular shape of the white glass container. The rose is a circular shape too.

Container: A white glass container on a wooden stand.

Materials: Plastic rods, Roses (Mon Cheri) and Angel Hair.

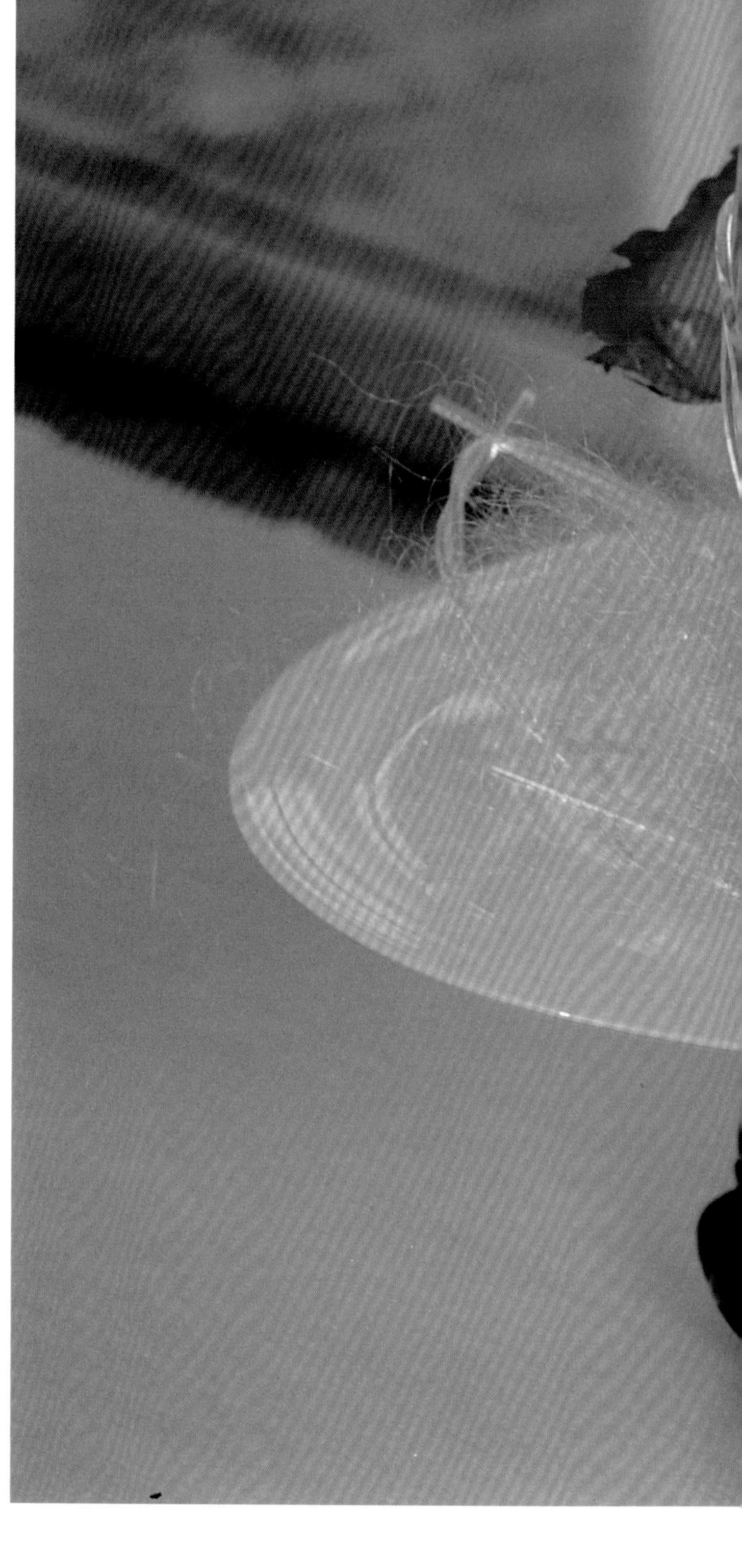

Different shades of the colour blue feature here. The purple/blue of the Iris flower contrasted with the blue of the billiard table, the blue water in the swimming pool and the blue water in the lake.
Iris, the vibrant purple/blue flower, is the flower used in Japan for Boys' Day Festival on May 5th. It signifies strength and masculinity. This vigorous, vibrant flower has become associated with males in Ikebana. However, women like it too! In this billiard room it seems very appropriate. The white glass container acted as a cool foil for the Iris. The striped grass gave a feeling of wind in the fields. The white-dotted Gypsophila was used to soften the arrangement.

Container: A glass container.

Materials: Striped Grass, Iris, Gypsophila.

This Ikebana is a celebration of the Sun. The golden-coloured container reinforces the colour and round shape of the Sun. This happy arrangement featured a "mass" arrangement of golden Roses (Helmut Schmidt). The Pine is symbolic of long life. The vine added interesting "line" to the mass.

Container: A golden container made from wood.

Materials: Pine, Roses (Helmut Schmidt) and Vine.

This Ikebana and container showed happiness, intimacy and love.

Yellow is the colour of joy. If a loved one is away, the loop of the wire and in this case the loop of the yellow container, conveys the wish for a safe return. The gold and silver wire is often used for Weddings and celebrations in Japan. In the West we often wrap our special gifts using gold and silver ribbon too. With just one Rose we have a beautiful arrangement.

Container: A ceramic container.

Materials: Gold and silver wire, Yellow Rose (Helmut Schmidt), yellow Angel Hair.

Bathrooms are very important rooms in the home. When we have time, the bath-tub is a great place in which to relax. This modern bathroom has a black and white colour scheme. The interesting Ikebana container is black with coloured dots. The Button Dahlias match well with the dots on the container. The coloured dots added impact to the overall black and white theme. The fresh, crisp green of the clipped palm leaves added an important design addition. The Button Dahlias added warmth to a cold bathroom. This would be a nice touch in winter.

Container: A ceramic container.

Materials: Clipped palm, Button Dahlia.

Use has been made of colour and flowers to complement the setting. The shape of the white container harmonises with the shape of the place-mats. The modern feeling has been enhanced by both the container and the materials used – such as the mirrored steel. The table arrangement is not too tall to see over. The Ikebana is interesting and decorative as a result.

Container: A white ceramic container.

Materials: Carnations, Gypsophila, Mirrored Steel.

This versatile container is always an interesting one to use. The Iris flowers have been massed for effect and the Spear grass has been curved over and incorporated into the mass. In the evening, this Ikebana comes into its own. The vibrant colours of the Iris add life and interest to this area of the home.

Container: A ceramic container.

Materials: Blackboy Grass and Iris.

This container is a Korean "Celadon" one. It is prized for its colour and glaze. Celadon is thought to be the colour of Good Luck. This Ikebana arrangement combines good luck and long life, by using Celadon (good luck) and Pine (long life). Red is the colour used for celebration and happy occasions. The Australian Gum-nuts added a touch of whimsy.

Container: A Korean Celadon container.

Materials: Pine, Carnation and Australian Gum-nuts.

MANSION

Creativity is important in Ikebana, as it is in other forms of Art, Music, Dance, Literature.

It is important for us to develop our own individual style.
To assist us in developing our own individual style, thought must be given to design, colour, balance and form. We have to learn how to best express our ideas.
Design – Design in modern Ikebana requires both imagination and craftsmanship.
Balance – Asymmetrical balance is stressed.
Colour – The three primary colours are yellow, red and blue. All other colours are formed by mixing these colours, except white and black. Colour can also be dominant or quiet, an important element or an unimportant element. From all the many colours of the rainbow, a choice must be made.
Form – The structure is important in Ikebana, as it is in building a house. Unless the form-work is right the house will not be built correctly.

The theme of this Ikebana arrangement in the Entrance is one of elegance. The large area has been balanced with a large arrangement. The ceramic container is tall. The style is refined, without appearing massive. The lofty ceilings have been balanced by the size of the Ikebana.
The smell of the Pine added a freshness to the area.
The purple Perennial Statice added a splash of colour, as did the white Seacrest. The bamboo, the symbol of flexibility, added height.

Container: A ceramic container.

Materials: Pine, Bamboo, Gold Twigs, Statice and Seacrest.

Ikebana has great appeal. This photo shows a demonstration I gave to two hundred and fifty people. We are always interested in finding out ways to improve our homes, no matter how big or small. The proceeds of this demonstration went to the local hospital.

As a minimum of elements had been used, each was carefully chosen for the role it had to play in the completed design. The container came from the same island in the Mediterranean as the owner & builder of this magnificent home had come from. The Cycad's leaves had been curved to reveal the interesting geometrical patterns. The Gerberas were used as a centre of interest.

The Lotus is a symbol of elegance, purity, immortality, propriety, sincerity & nobleness.

The Lotus is thought to be the most pure flower, because the plant's roots grow in mud, but the plant grows towards heaven and the flowers are exquisite. The analogy is that no matter where we were born or our background, we can rise above it. The green lotus shape of the container emphasised the water theme.
In this room the spa was bubbling & frothing. The Ikebana was designed to harmonise with the setting. The flowers are called "Love in the Mist". The flowers combined well with the leaves of the Iris and illustrated the invigorating water theme. Looking at the Ikebana made one think of bathing in a greenery. In a city house this arrangement would provide an element of escapism in everyday life.

Container: A ceramic container.

Materials: Iris, Love in the Mist.

THE FARM COTTAGE

"Mountains of green, mountains of blue arise: My gratitude wells up and fills my eyes"

A Haiku poem by Ho-o.

The Hinterland is a beautiful area of the Gold Coast. Distant views of blue hills to the West, the coastline to the East. There are many areas of wonderful mountain walks, rainforest, waterfalls and tree-ferns.

There is a fascinating, true story of this area, and I tell it because I love a good story and also because it illustrates not only the perseverance and inventiveness of Australians of the past, but also the qualities that have been shared and passed on to our generation. These qualities influence our Ikebana and strengthen us as individuals.

An aeroplane crashed into the densely wooded hillside, many years ago, when flight was in its infancy. The newspapers of the time carried the story until all hope seemed to fade. Not many people lived in this area at that time. One local man believed he could find the aeroplane. He took a donkey, axe and supplies and cut his way through the thick undergrowth. This took many days and the days were beginning to be counted in weeks, when he saw something glinting in the far distance! It was the sun glinting on the wing of the aeroplane. He had lost all hope of finding anyone alive. It took him another couple of days to reach the aeroplane and propped up against the wing was the pilot, who looked like a living skeleton, but was alive! The pilot said to his rescuer "I knew someone would come!"

How lucky he was that someone had the perseverance to push on through such wild, untouched country.

I believe we have the perseverance to learn the Art of Ikebana and the individuality to excel at it.

This is a well thought-out arrangement, but one that conveys the freedom of the bush. This lovely little cottage is definitely a home, complete with an attic and lovely old black dog!

The arrangement has a feeling of country charm. The container is rustic in feeling. The Goldenrod (bright yellow flower) is happy and warm in colour. Goldenrod is said to be one of the brightest features of North American woodlands in late summer. The striped grass matches well with the grass in the field. The Weeping Mulberry branch has not been used in its weeping form. Flowers or branches that droop down give a sad feeling. The Mulberry branch has been used in this way to add movement and dynamic shape to the arrangement. The space left emphasises the form.

Container: A Raku fired container.

Materials: Mulberry branch, Striped Grass, Goldenrod (Solidago).

I approached this arrangement with the attitude that country arrangements must not always be old-fashioned. Modern Ikebana fits into a rustic setting easily. The striking line of the iron (which had been found on the farm) was used in order to bring out the interesting design on the container. This arrangement incorporated unconventional material. The Poinciana Tree has interesting pods, when flowering is finished. I introduced the Poinciana Pods into the arrangement as a feature, which complemented the iron and acted as a foil for the focal accent of the Aster or Michaelmas or Easter Daisy.

The lines used in the Ikebana contrasted with the regular lines of the walls, floor and posts of the farm cottage.

Container: A ceramic container.

Materials: Iron, Poinciana Pods and Aster or Michaelmas or Easter Daisy.

Isn't this a wonderful sunset?

The Ikebana sits like a bright gem in this area. I was born in a country area and barbed-wire is very much a part of country life and farm fences. I can remember as a little girl getting my skirt caught in the barbed wire while running home from school. I worried what my mother would say about the big tear! The barbed wire in this arrangement forms an interesting base. It anchors the arrangement and imbues it with a country feeling. The American Cotton Palm provides a fan-like backdrop. It reminds us that we live in a tropical area. The Geranium (Pelargonium) has been used as vibrant, glowing colour. I think every farm in Australia and New Zealand would have a Geranium growing in the garden. The colour and shape of the container and the colour of the Geranium is in harmony with the setting sun.

Container: A ceramic container, with an unusual glaze.

Materials: American Cotton Palm, Geranium (Pelargonium), Barbed Wire.

HOME WITH VIEWS OF THE GOLD

This beautiful home is said by the owner "to have the best views of the Gold Coast". It seemed to be a fitting end to a book entitled "Ikebana at Home."

The skyline of the Gold Coast can be seen in the distance, in the light of the setting sun.

The rich, red colour of the Anthurium brings to mind the sun & the tropics & modern Ikebana. Notice that an odd number of Anthurium flowers has been used. Five & seven are lucky numbers. The Anthuriums used in this arrangement grow in profusion near the front door of this home! The squiggles on this interesting container bring to mind the Strangler Vine of the rainforest. A piece of twisted Strangler Vine has been used in the composition. The healthy, dark-green surface of the Anthurium leaf adds a clean, healthy feature to this arrangement. The pine, of course, is to wish you a long, happy & successful life.

Container: A ceramic container.

Materials: A piece of Strangler Vine, Anthurium flowers & leaf, Pine.

COAST

EQUIPMENT USED IN IKEBANA

There is a wide range of Ikebana equipment available from my Ikebana centre. A choice should be made to suit the container, pocket and arrangement.

1. Kenzans or needle point holders. These range from tiny to very large. They usually last a life time. The green-coloured Kenzans are more easily concealed in the water. Cheaper locally made Kenzans are a problem because the spikes are too far apart. Some Kenzans come in their own metal container.
2. The Shippo type of Kenzan supports heavy branches. The acrylic twist is a glass Kenzan, and supports branches in clear glass containers.
3. Kenzan Straightener and Cleaner.
4. Angel Hair.Comes in various colours, and can be re-used.
5. Hasami or clippers. The smaller ones fit in the hand well and should last for many years. They are specially balanced for use in one hand. The larger clippers are for heavy branches. There are also Hasami covers.
6. The rolls of iridescent paper are used in arrangements which feature water.
7. The glass pebbles are used in arrangements which also feature water.
8. The small saw is handy for heavy branches.
9. There are many different shades of coloured wires.
10. Plastic rods.
11. Sets of Ikebana tools.
12. Coloured paper rolls.
13. Floral tape.

Paper Ribbon

SELECTION OF CONTAINERS

The choice of container is very important in Ikebana – because it becomes as one with the whole composition. It doesn't just hold water – it completes the arrangement.

Therefore you must choose it with care.

The shape, the colour and the design are very important.

A highly decorated container should be avoided – because a plainer one sets off the flowers to greater advantage.

Think about the space where you are going to place your Ikebana.

A too small container might not suit, just as one too large might overwhelm. If you have large rooms – large Ikebana will suit you. If you have smaller rooms – or spaces for Ikebana – smaller containers are in proportion with the space available.

There are three types of Ikebana containers:

1. Moribana.

Moribana containers are low containers & come in two categories – Basic Moribana Containers & Advanced Moribana Containers. Basic Moribana Containers are of a basic shape & size. Advanced Moribana Containers are low containers, however have something different about them e.g. shape, design or colour.

For Moribana a wide & low vase is suitable. Moribana can best display its beauty in a large vase.

2. Nageire.

Nageire are tall containers & come in two categories – Basic Nageire Containers & Advanced Nageire Containers. The Basic Nageire Containers are of basic shape & height. Advanced Nageire Containers, however, have something different about them e.g. added height, unusual design, or unusual colour. For Nageire a tall, slender vase is used, because the inner sides of the vase are used for support.

MORIBANA CONTAINERS.

3. Free-style or Creative Containers.

Free-style containers are creative containers, which suit such things as special occasions,seasons of the year, times of the year. They can have a modern feeling or be elegant, quiet, loud, noisy, peaceful, understated, dramatic etc. The choice of container depends upon the feeling & mood you want to convey.

There are many different shapes – square, rectangular, cylindrical, compote, hanging style, asymmetrical etc.
Containers are made from many different materials, such as bamboo, plastic, wood, glass, stone, pottery, iron, bronze, etc. Each produces a different effect.
After using containers, we must clean them.
We must also care for our tools. Ikebana is only completed when the materials & tools have been properly cleaned & put away.

NAGEIRE CONTAINERS.

FREE-STYLE OR CREATIVE CONTAINERS.

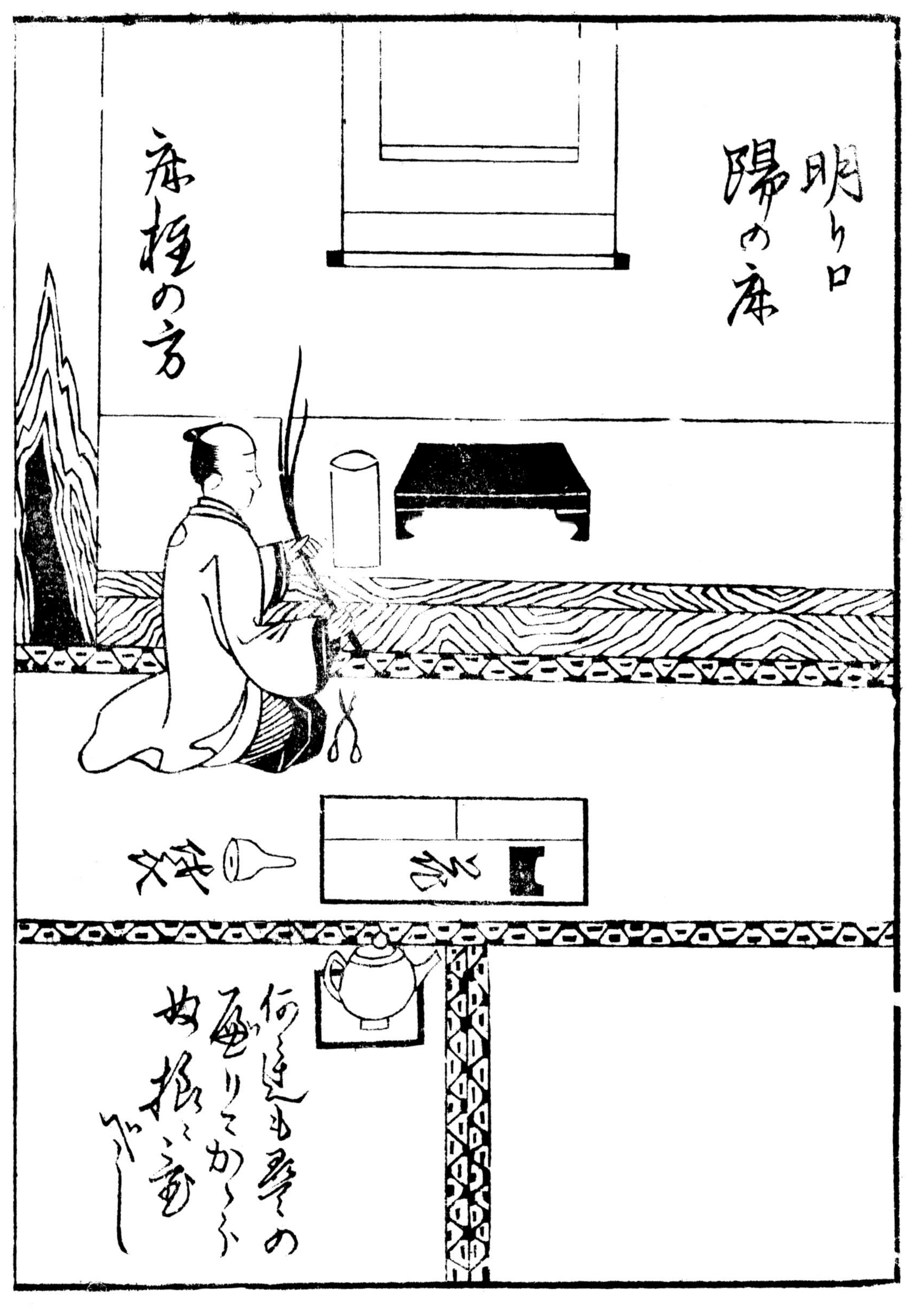

This picture of a man doing Ikebana was taken from an old Ikebana book titled KAJUTSU SENSAI NO MAKI - 1868.

CONCEPTS OF IKEBANA

A Brief History of the three leading Schools of Ikebana in Japan, The Ikenobo School, The Ohara School and The Sogetsu School.

Obviously Ancient China influenced Japan strongly. Just as we in the West were influenced by Ancient Egypt, Ancient Greece and Ancient Rome.

Ikenobo History.

In the 6th Century, Ono no Imoko paid three official visits to the Imperial court of China. After his retirement he was appointed guardian of Rokkaku-do, a Buddhist temple in Kyoto. There he became abbot, changed his name to Senmu and lived in a small house known as the ike-no-bo or "the hut by the pond". In China he had studied arranging flowers as religious offerings, and in retirement he continued to develop his study of the way of the flowers. From this has developed Japan's oldest school of Ikebana. The Ikenobo school has a 1400 year tradition as its heritage. I have studied many times at the Ikenobo School in Kyoto. I teach Ikenobo Ikebana and Sogetsu Ikebana.

Ohara History.

The Ohara School of Ikebana dates back to the Meji Period (1867-1912). Unshin Ohara arrived in Osaka with the ambition to be a sculptor. His health was not good and because of his early training in the Ikenobo School of flower arranging he turned his energies to Ikebana. The Ikenobo School seemed to him too rigid and formal. Also Western flowers were beginning to appear in Japan. He greatly admired them and wished to use them in flower arrangements. Thus he decided to make his own type of flower arrangements in tray-like containers called suiban, which he had made for this purpose. Not only did he find a new way of using different flowers, he started the modern moribana type of arrangement, which shocked the classical teachers of the time. Unshin died in 1916 and was succeeded by his son Koun, who died in 1938. His son Houn is the present headmaster of the Ohara School. I watched his demonstration in Tokyo in 1991 and even though a very old man, his Ikebana is still wonderful.

Sogetsu History.

Sofu Teshigahara was born in Tokyo in 1907. He learnt flower-arranging from his father who had studied many styles of different schools. When he was twenty-five he was ready to start the Sogetsu School of Ikebana. He believed that we must make modern arrangements for the places where we live. He believed that Ikebana is not merely decorating with flowers, it is an Art. That the great difference between floral decoration and Ikebana lies in the belief that once all the rules are learnt, the techniques mastered, we must sculpt. Thus we create living sculptures.

I had the honour to meet both Sofu and his daughter and intended-successor Kasumi, before their deaths. Kasumi's brother Hiroshi Teshigahara is now Headmaster of the Sogetsu School. I visit the Sogetsu School often and teach Sogetsu Ikebana. Many famous people have visited the Sogetsu School for Ikebana lessons, such as Queen Elizabeth II, Princess Diana, Mrs Gandhi and many others.

The Moriband Style

In the Sogetsu School there are two basic styles, the Moribana and Nageire styles. The Moribana is the easier of the two because a kenzan or needle-point holder is used.

Moribana is seen as the freest and most expressive of the Ikebana styles. Line and colour are the two elements insisted upon. "If, " said Sofu Teshigahara, "you are particularly struck by an arrangement and find it full of beauty, then you may be certain that this arrangement has successfully combined line and colour." "A beautiful combination of beautiful lines, results in beautiful form", once this form is complete the colours will enrich and vitalise it.

The first step in learning Ikebana is to learn and master the Moribana style. Lesson books are available. I have included Lesson 1. Moribana style, for those who are new to Ikebana. Also following is a lesson in the Nageire style.

Nature often dictates how plants should be arranged in the Moribana style. Some need to be upright, while others need a steeply slanting style and while still others, such as the Wisteria, need a cascading line. Iris looks best when gathered at the base and spread out, while other plants need to be arranged more loosely at the base.

The aim is to bring out the natural beauty of the flowers or branches used, just as if they were still growing in the field.

We must show our own love of nature in this arrangement.

The Ikebana in this picture is the basic upright form of Moribana. In this lesson Magnolia (with new Spring leaves) and Azalea have been used. Magnolia with new growth and Azalea are both plants redolent of Spring. Spring has the feeling of new life, hope and joy. Freshness and simplicity are emphasised in the lines of this arrangement. The expanse of water is important. It's as if a soft, gentle breeze is gently moving the fresh leaves of the Magnolia and blowing over the Azalea and rippling the surface of the small pond.

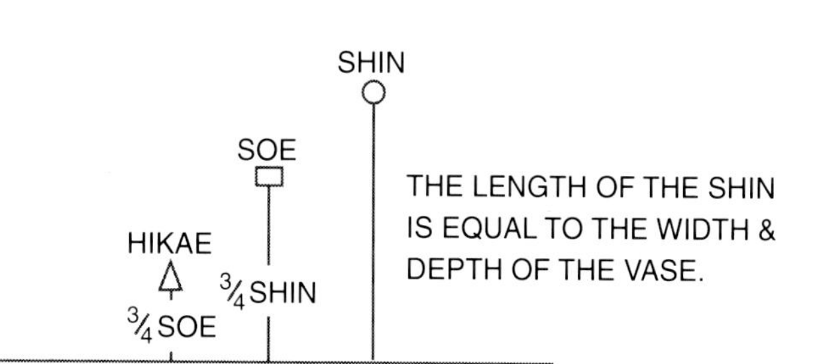

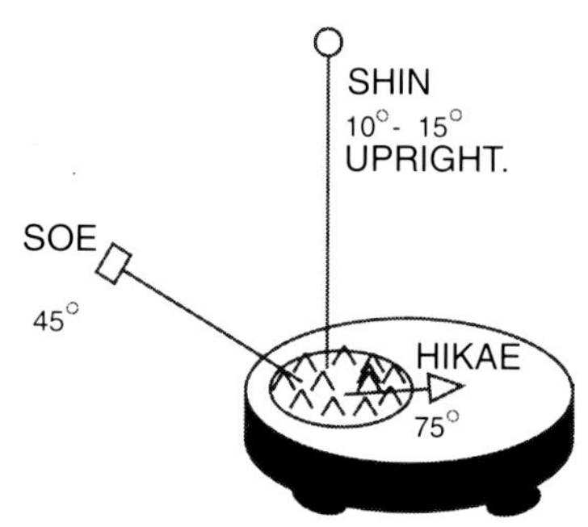

The Nageire Style

Nageire is a style arranged in a tall narrow-mouthed container, rather than a low one with a broad expanse of water showing.
Nageire requires more skill in fixing the materials in place. There are two different approaches in the Sogetsu School. One stresses naturalness and is called the naturalistic approach. This approach stresses how the branch grows in nature and the natural individuality of the plant is revealed. The second approach stresses the human element, showing the individual personality of the person arranging the Ikebana. Each of these approaches is always present in every arrangement, to a lesser or greater degree.
Flowers are not always beautiful. In a florist's they are often in rough bunches. When we bring them in from the garden they often show more defects, than reveal their beauty. The stems must always be trimmed, the leaves removed for those stems eventually under water. The beauty of the remaining part must stand for the ideal beauty of the whole. It is like polishing and cutting a rough stone to reveal a beautiful gem. It is important to recognise whether the emphasis is upon the individual or on the flower. Either is the result of the search for ideal beauty.
I would like to show you the basic slanting style of Nageire. The Moribana was upright, this Nageire is slanting, because the Shin branch is slanting.

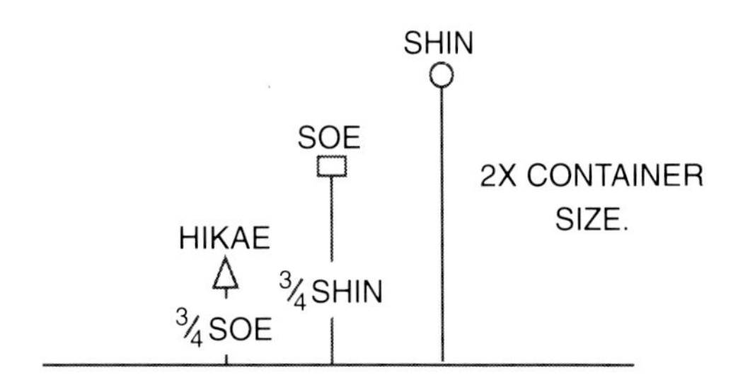

In the slanting form the lines are important, as shown in this arrangement. The incline depends upon the materials used and the rules of good composition. The proportions are, in general: the length of shin is twice the container size, soe is 3/4 of shin and hikae is 3/4 of soe. In my arrangement, I have used Macadamia Nut branches. Macadamia Nuts are native to Queensland, Australia. Two of the branches were of Japonica. The new life and new shoots belonged to

the Japonica. Spring was on its way. The tiny branches were from the palm tree and were used as auxiliary branches. The beautiful Phalaenopsis Orchids were all growing on one stem and so were brought forward towards the viewer (the sun). The branches were the shin and soe and the Orchids were the hikae.

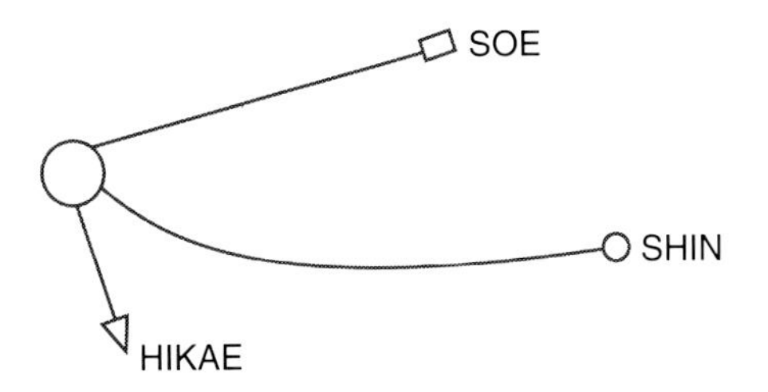

It is important to have flexible attitudes towards the material's features. We must check that everything is in harmony, is well balanced and that the whole arrangement has unity.

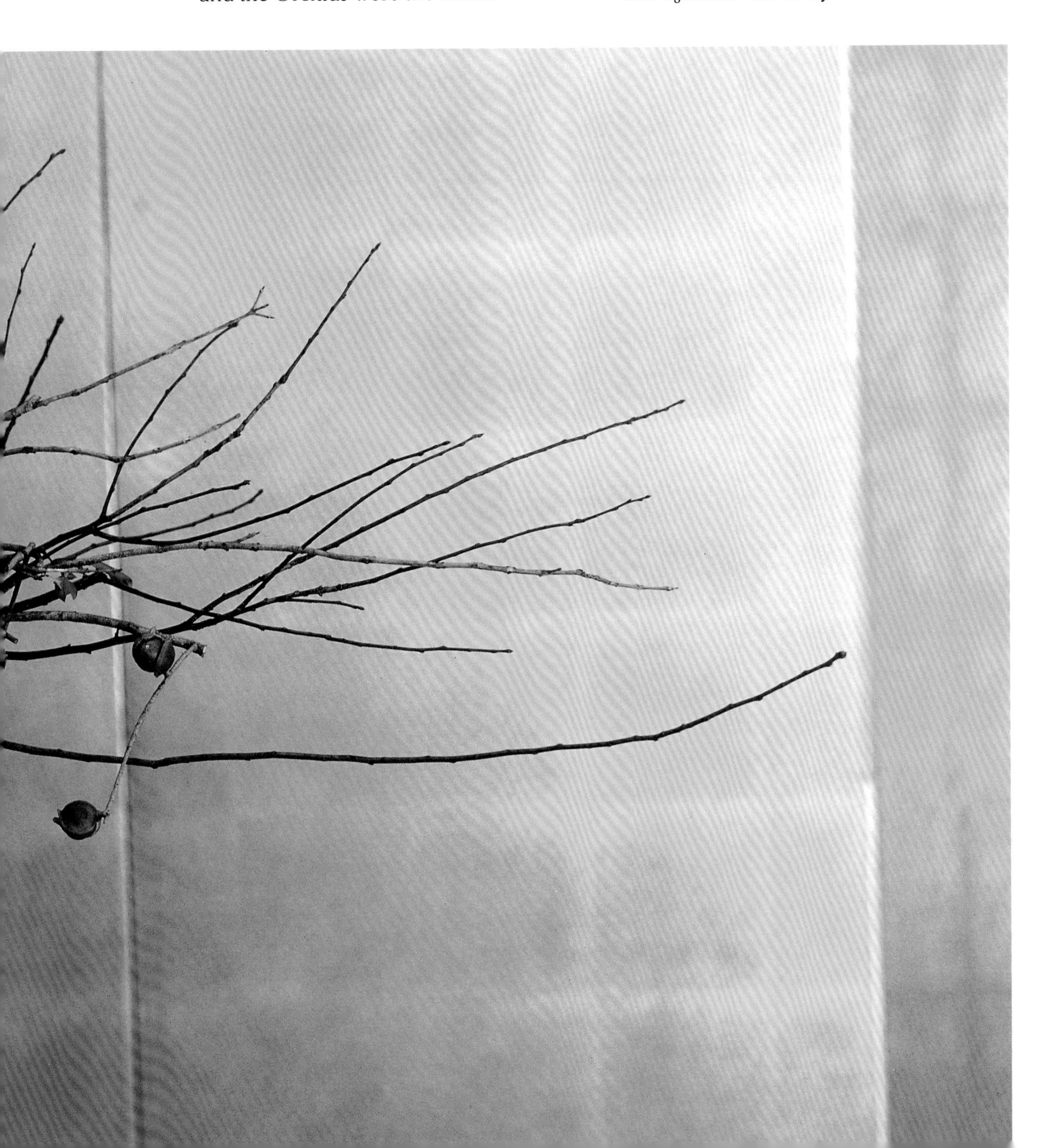

Cutting and Trimming

After selection of a suitable branch, which best fits our arrangement, we must prepare it before arranging. Unneeded parts of the branch are removed with hasami or ikebana scissors or a saw. Leaves are trimmed and smaller unwanted branches removed. I often place the branch in the kenzan to see how it will look in the arrangement before using it and while trimming it. Often the branch is shaped by bending. By bending, the curve can be accentuated or straightened out, thus giving the branch more extension.

Thin stems or soft-stemmed material can be cut using the tip of the hasami. Thick branches must be cut at an angle. After cutting the thick branch on an angle the tip of the branch must be cut off to make a blunt end. The cut end of the branch is given several short cuts so that the branch is easily inserted into the kenzan. Water can be drawn up into the branch and it will preserve its freshness longer with this method. Place the branch firmly into the kenzan, before bending to the desired angle. The branch may fall out or be unstable if you attempt to place it on

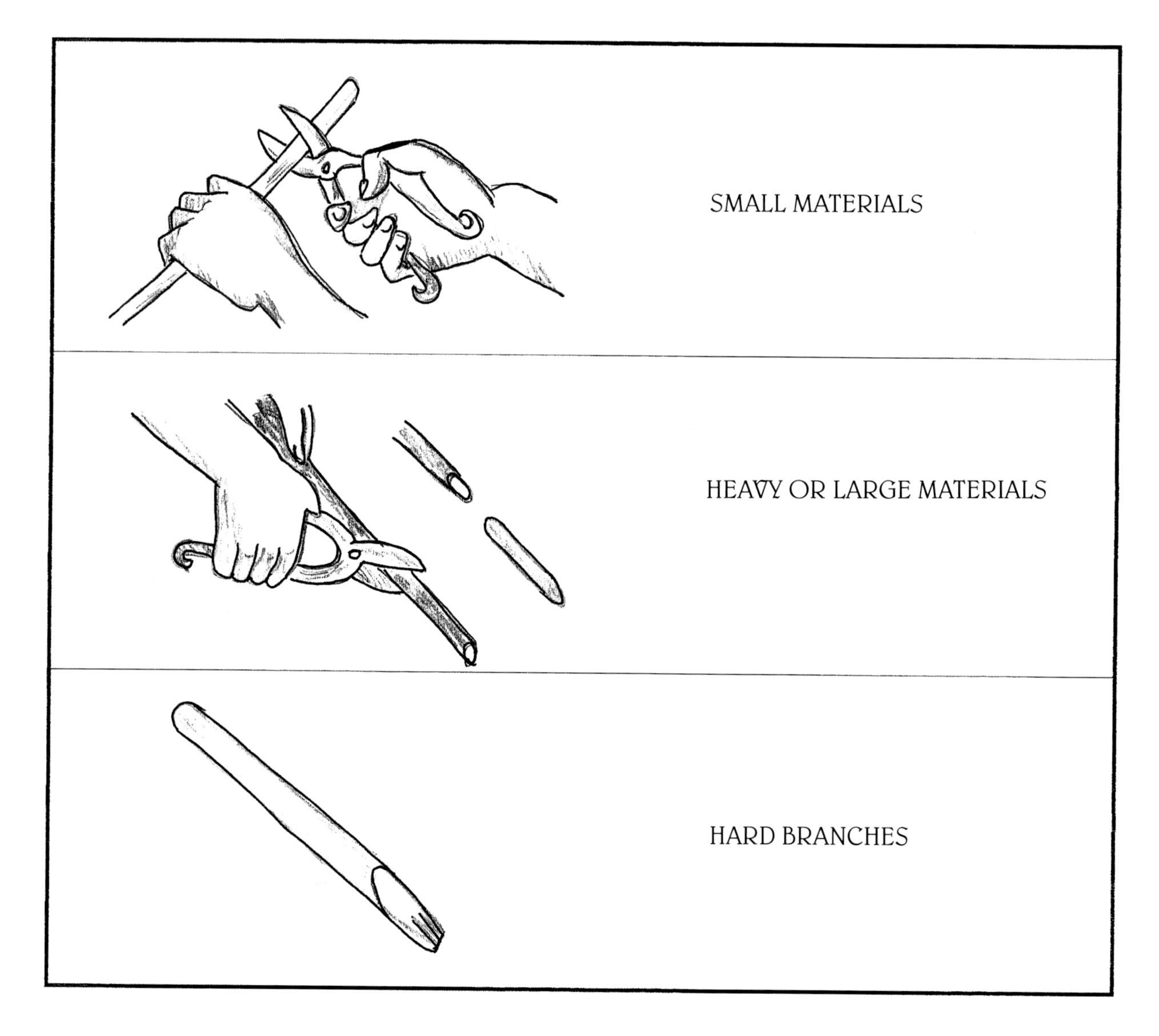

the kenzan at an angle. Cut all leaves off under the water level, as these foul the water.

Removing Branches.
Often trimming is necessary to bring out the beauty of the material and to produce the desired design. Removal of just one branch can produce a startling change for the better. The tips of branches often need careful manicuring. Small twigs at the base are usually removed. Remove one of two branches that point in the same direction. Also remove one branch if two are about the same shape or height. If two branches cross, remove one. If a branch comes too close to another remove it. Any good arrangement emphasises the space it contains and branches can be removed to create this effect.

Removing Leaves.
In general, woody branches with many leaves need more drastic trimming than flowery branches. Also, if the branch is in flower, too many leaves would detract from the flowers, so more leaves should be removed. However, some sections of the branch should be left dense while others should be thinned out.

Removing Flowers.
We desire harmony between the flowers and the leaves and branches. Therefore, flowers that detract from the overall effect should be removed. Also, spent flowers should be removed.

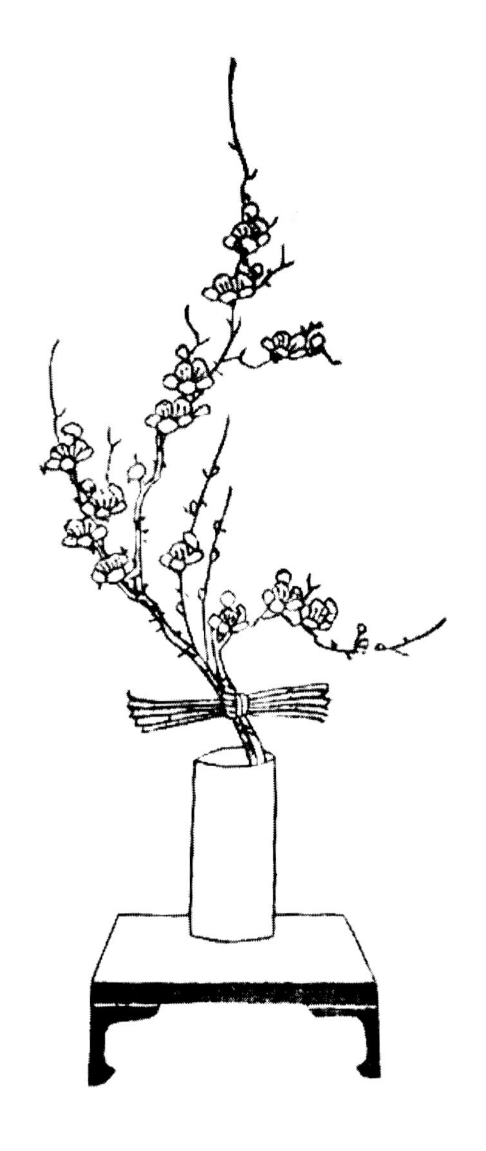

This picture taken from KAJUTSU SENSAI NO MAKI - 1868, shows why bending, cutting and trimming are necessary. Beautiful curved, sweeping and cascading shapes can be achieved by bending, cutting and trimming.

Bending

Often we must bend or straighten branches. Some are easy to bend while others are difficult and break easily. Choose one of the following methods, depending on the material used. Continued practice is necessary.

1. Bending by twisting.
Hard and easily broken material is often made more pliable by twisting. Twist with both hands and at the same time add force by bending.

2. Bending by pushing.
Support the branch with both hands, the thumbs close together, and gradually bend the branch. For a very thick branch, anchor one end and gradually bend the branch by pulling upward.

3. Bending by cutting.
A thick stem can be bent successfully by making a small cut less than halfway through the stem. The branch is then bent at the place of the cut. Apply force gradually.

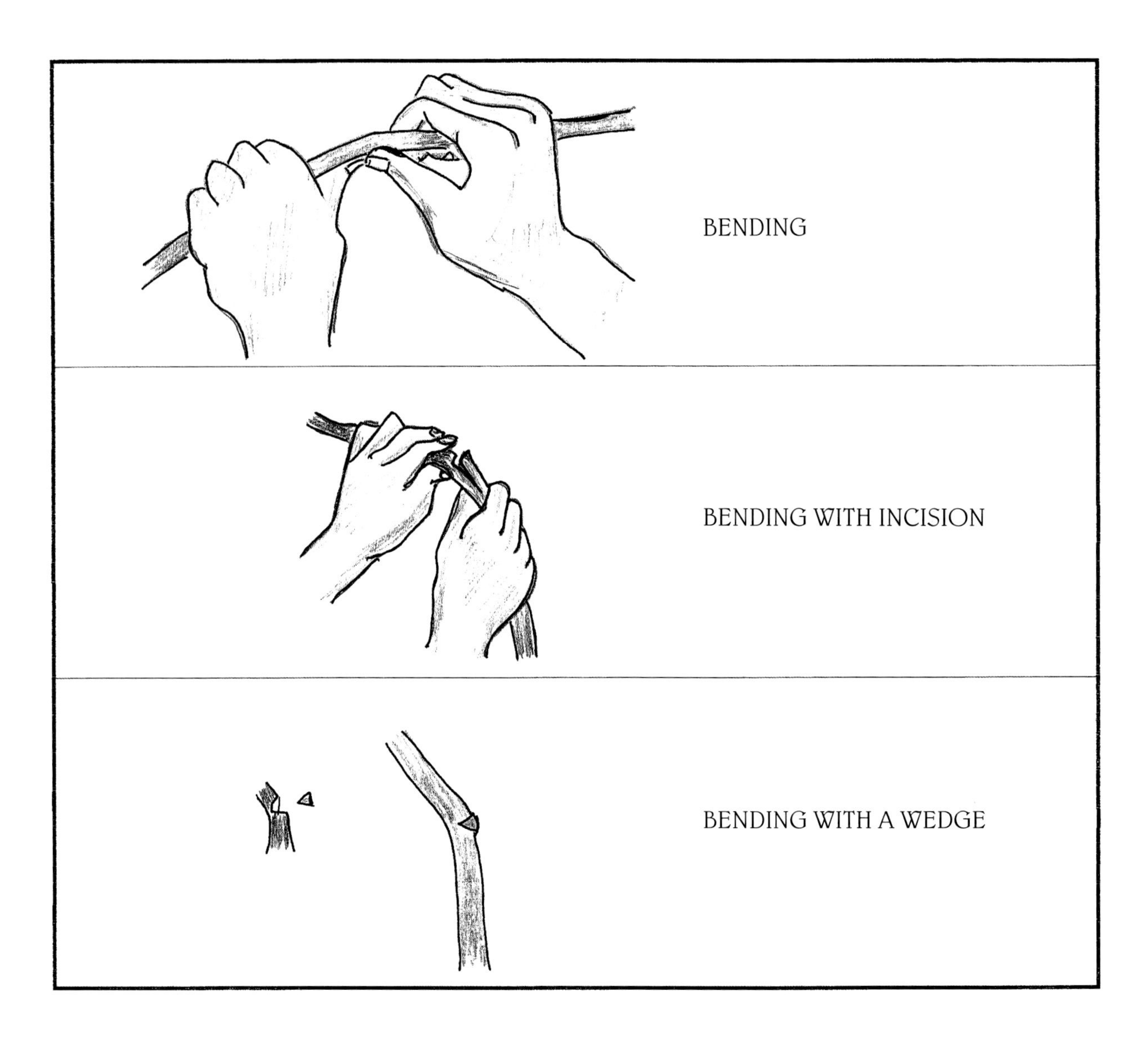

4. Bending by drawing through the fingers or hand.

A curve can be given to leaves by pressing on the leaf and gently drawing the leaf through the fingers. The warmth of the fingers gently curves the leaf plus the gentle pressure.

5. Bending by inserting a wedge.

For a very thick branch such as Pine, make a cut where a bend is required. Do not cut too deeply. Bend the branch slowly and carefully and insert a wedge of the same material into the cut. The branch will retain its bend in this way.

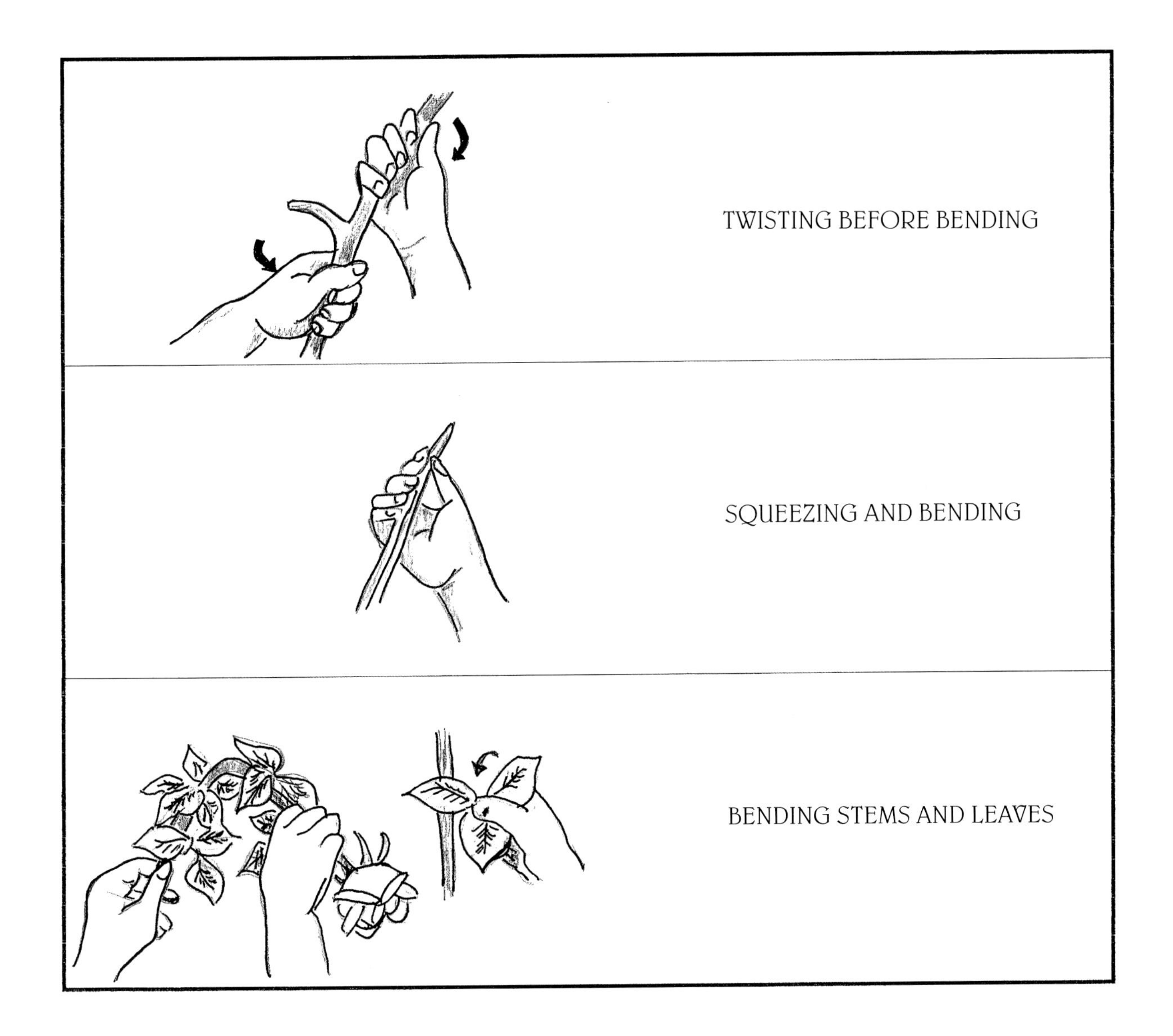

Fixing in Place

Moribana depends upon a kenzan to fix in place.
Nageire demands more complicated methods

The Kenzan Method of fixing material in place.

Hard branches: Cut on an angle and not straight across. Blunt the end. The cut end should have a number of cuts, in order to be able to insert the branch easily in the kenzan. Also, water is drawn up more easily into the stem by using this method. If you want the branch to slant, first stand it upright on the kenzan and then bring it down to the desired angle, pressing the bark onto the needles.

Softer branches: Cut horizontally. There are a number of methods we can use if a slender stem does not fit on the kenzan.

(a) wrap a piece of paper or leaf around the base.
(b) splice it to a larger twig or
(c) insert it into a larger stem.

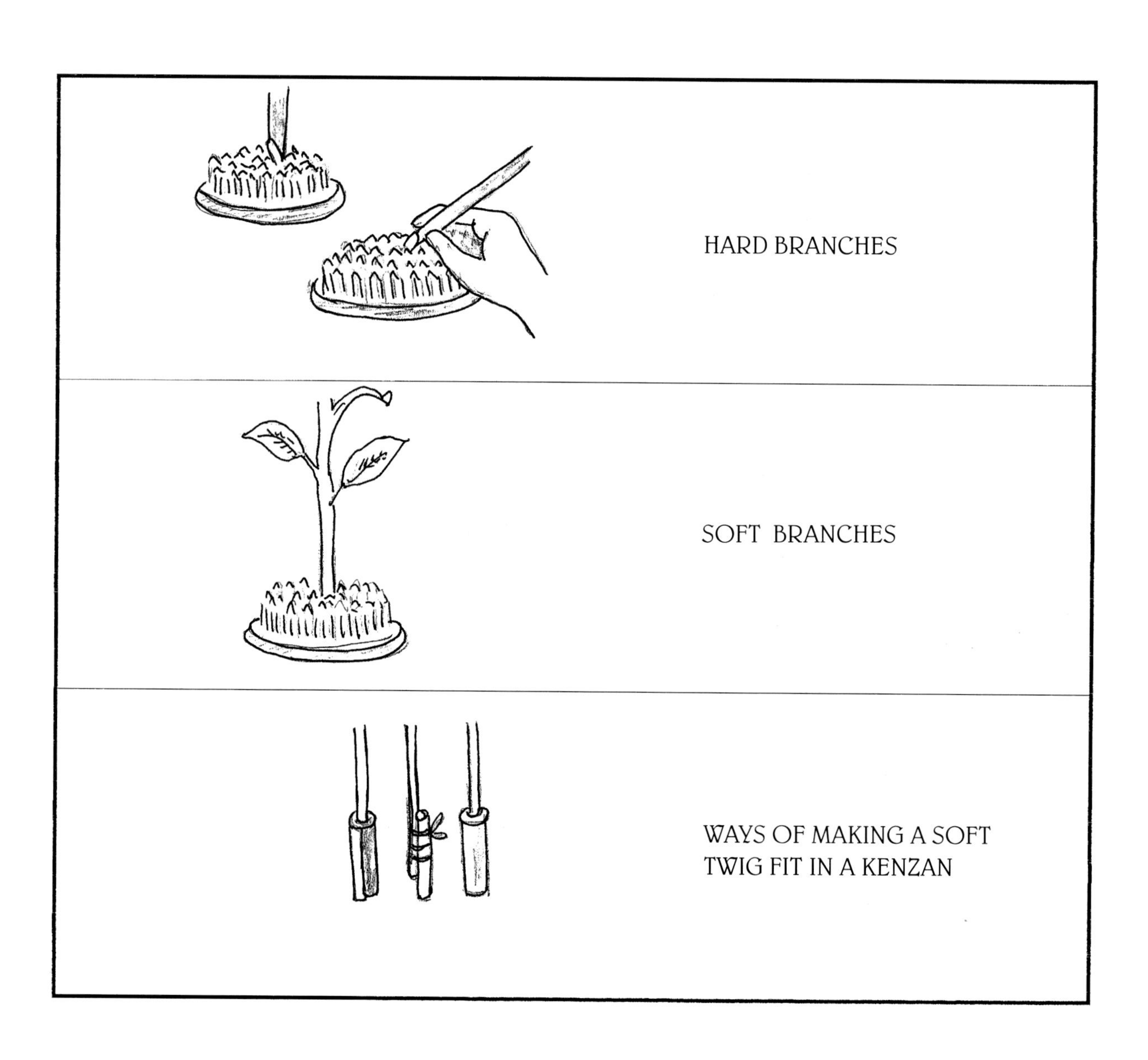

The Nageire method of fixing in place.

1. The cross-bar method.
Two twigs are cut to fit into the mouth of the vase in the shape of a cross. Branches are then usually inserted in only one of the four quarters. Be careful not to break the containers by using this method. Some containers have rings at the top inside to help with this method.

2. Down-stick method.
This method is useful in all kinds of vases. The down-stick may stand upright away from the wall of the vase or it can lean on the wall for support. Both the branch and the down-stick are split and placed firmly together. They can be tied if necessary.

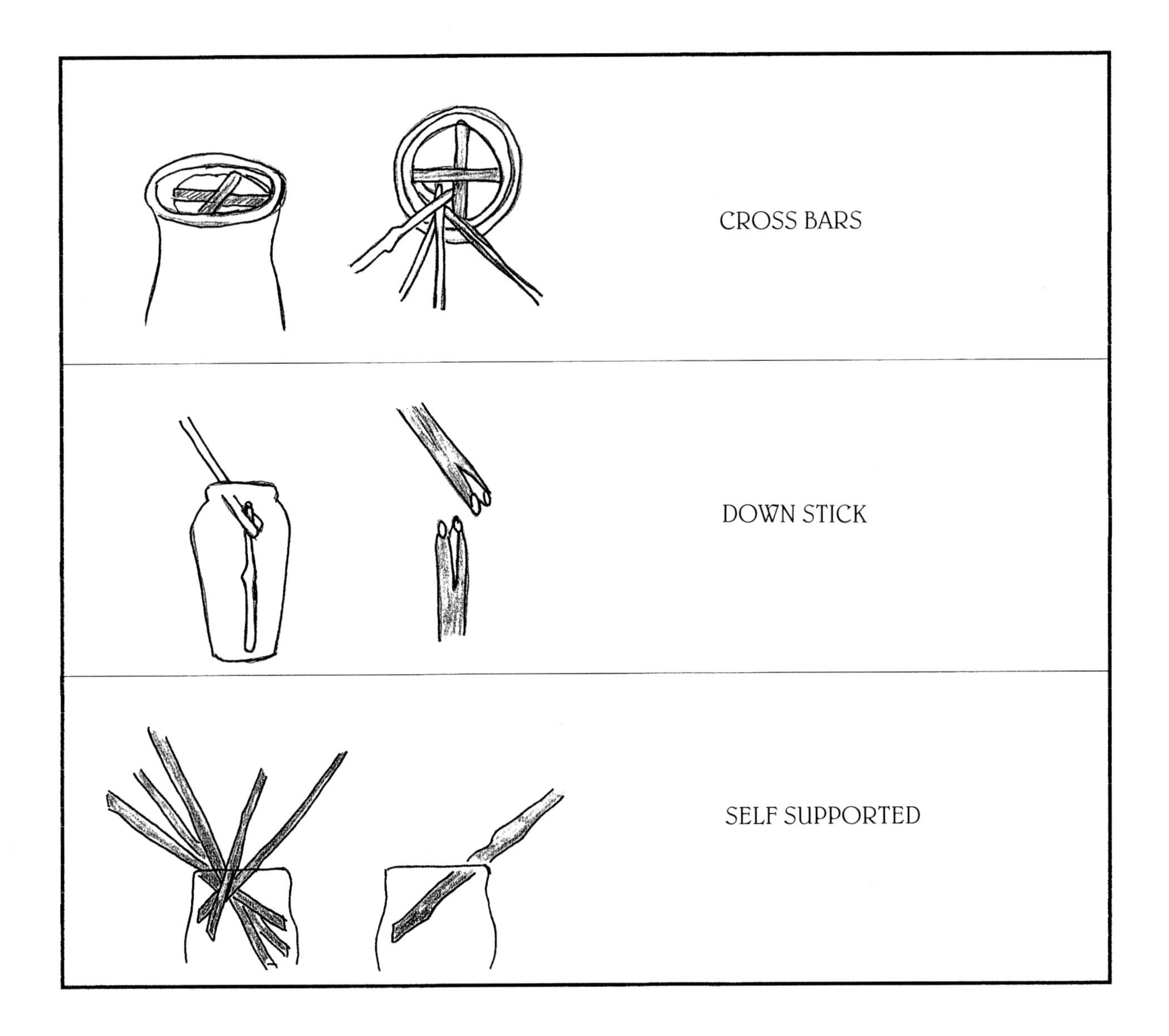

Preserving Plant Material

I think this is a very important part of the book, because we do not want our arrangement to wilt and droop too quickly! The preservation of plant material is an essential part of Ikebana. Over the centuries the Japanese have devised a number of methods of preservation. I will discuss a number of methods here and then list briefly how some of the plant material used in this book had been treated.

1. Cutting under water.
If we cut stems under water, we prevent air from entering and the plant is able to more readily absorb water. Cut the stems under water until time to use. Then re-cut under water, in a bowl of water. This seals the cut end.

2. Crushing or cutting the stem.
Plants can be preserved by
a) crushing or pounding the stem.
b) by cutting the stem on an angle.
c) splitting the end of the stem into two or three small parts.

3. Burning the stem.
With any stem containing a milky substance, burning works well.
Burn the ends over a flame or dip in boiling water.

4. A water pump.
Plants such as water lilies need special care.
Fluid is injected into the stem. The fluid can be:
a) water.
b) one teaspoon of alum to a quart of cold water.
c) tobacco juice, which is made by soaking cigarettes in water and straining.
d) ginger water, which is made by boiling fresh scraped ginger root and allowing to cool.
e) cold tea.

5. Chemicals.
a) Dip in peppermint oil.
b) Dip in alcohol.

This is by no means a complete list of how to preserve plant material, however it will be of help.

Anthurium: cut in water.
Gypsophila: cut in water.
Bamboo: for big bamboo, open hole at a node and pour in salt water, for small, dip in vinegar.
Bougainvillaea: dip in peppermint oil.
Camellia: cut in water.
Carnation: cut in water.
Peony: burn the cut end.
Chrysanthemum: cut in water.
Crepe Myrtle: cut in water.
Dracaena: none needed.
Eucalyptus (Blue Gum): cut in water.
Gardenia: cut in water or dip in alcohol.
Geranium: cut in water.
Gerbera: cut in water or dip in peppermint oil.
Hibiscus: dip in alcohol or cut in water.
Iris: cut in water.
Lily: cut in water.
Lotus: inject thinly diluted acetic acid into stem with pump, or dip cut end into water from the pond in which the lotus grew.
Orchid: cut in water.
Palm: none needed.
Pine: none needed.
Pussy willow: none needed.
Rose: cut in water or burn the cut end.